THE GIFT OF STUTTERING

CONFRONTING LIFE'S CHALLENGES:

A PERSONAL JOURNEY

THE GIFT OF STUTTERING

CONFRONTING LIFE'S CHALLENGES:
A PERSONAL JOURNEY

Moe Mernick

MOSAICA PRESS

Mosaica Press, Inc.
© 2016 by Mosaica Press

Designed and typeset by Rayzel Broyde
All rights reserved
ISBN-10: 1937887588
ISBN-13: 978-1-937887-58-2

No part of this publication may be translated, reproduced, stored in a retrieval system or transmitted in any form or by any means, electronic, mechanical, photocopying, recording, or otherwise, without prior permission in writing from both the copyright holder and the publisher.

Published and distributed by:
Mosaica Press, Inc.
www.mosaicapress.com
info@mosaicapress.com

CONTENTS

Acknowledgments 7
Foreword 11
Introduction 19
Chapter 1 - Welcome to My Life 31
Chapter 2 - Growing Pains 47
Chapter 3 - Learning to Deal with Challenges 60
Chapter 4 - Becoming Happy with Myself 81
Chapter 5 - Taking Action 100
Chapter 6 - To Europe and Beyond 118
Chapter 7 - Dating, Marriage, and Family 143
Chapter 8 - Being the Change 162
Conclusion 172

Appendix 1 - Succinct Stuttering-Related Advice 182
Appendix 2 - Stuttering-Related Resources 186
Appendix 3 - Some Notable People Who Stutter(ed) 190
Appendix 4 - Did Moshe Rabbeinu Stutter? 195
Appendix 5 - Recommended Reading List 200
Appendix 6 - Crowdfunding Campaign 202

ACKNOWLEDGMENTS

BEHIND EVERY BOOK is an author, and behind every author is a story.

These pages tell much of mine. Yet perhaps what is less apparent are the people who helped me become the kind of person whose story would be published. As such, I would like to succinctly express my sincerest gratitude to the incredible people who helped this book become a reality.

My Rabbis and Mentors — Those of you who truly impacted me, you know who you are. I am forever indebted to you. You selflessly devoted yourself to my emotional and spiritual growth. During the hard times, you went above and beyond to keep me strong; and in the easier times, you knew how to encourage me to take the next steps. You cared for me and expressed that in all kinds of ways. Most importantly, though, you believed in me. You continuously reminded me of my uniqueness and true potential in this world. It is my hope that this book (and all that is behind it) will give you the strength to continue to inspire many more people.

My Friends — In all my travels, I have been privileged to become acquainted with many different kinds of people. Each of you have taught me so much — about positivity, about perseverance, and about tapping into our individuality to impact the world. Thank you. And to my closest friends, you gave me a shoulder to lean on, you listened when I just needed to cry, and you gave me hope for being the kind of person I've become. Thank you for demonstrating the importance and value of true friendship. I feel blessed to have you in my life, and it is my hope that I can be there as much for you as you have been there for me.

My Publisher — Rabbi Yaacov Haber, from our first conversation in your office, I knew that I wanted to publish my book with you. Your sincere, genuine interest in my story and vision for what it could do for the Jewish People made me feel confident enough to entrust my manuscript to you and your talented team. I am happy I did. Rabbi Doron Kornbluth, you helped transform my collection of thoughts into an organized, powerful book. You constantly made yourself available to me, ensuring that I delivered the finest finished product possible. And to the rest of the Mosaica Press team: Thank you for helping me achieve my dream of publishing such a professional and polished book. May G-d bless you in all areas of your lives.[1]

My Family — Eema (mother), it is clear that I wouldn't be who I am today if not for you. Therefore, on behalf of my wife, kids, and every reader of this book, thank you very much for that (and for your valuable time and editorial skills that helped this book become all that it could be!). Abba (father), your undivided love means the world to me. You have been a huge supporter of this book from the get-go and I have sincerely appreciated all of your encouragement along the way. Thank you very much for sincerely believing in me. To my siblings and siblings-in-law,

---

1 Throughout this book, G-d's name is spelled with a dash, "G-d." This is done as a sign of respect, in case the book is discarded or destroyed.

thank you for all those times you put up with me, stood up for me, and were proud of me. Please also know that your enthusiasm for this project really helped move it along. It is a privilege to be your brother. To my in-laws and sisters-in-law, I feel blessed to have become part of your family. Thank you for lovingly accepting me for who I am, stutter included. An additional note of gratitude to all those family members who spent time reviewing the manuscript, and provided invaluable insights and feedback.

My Wife and Children — To my dear wife, Melanie, words cannot properly express my gratitude for being your other half. Thank you for choosing me and for helping me be all that I can be. And please know: *"Sheli v'shelahem, shelah"* — all the credit that my readers and I receive for growing through this book accrues to you. To my children, perhaps the most genuine intention of this book — of this three-year project — has been to share my story with you. Please appreciate G-d's infinite wisdom and Judaism's inherent beauty, and channel your unique talents to impact the world in a way that nobody else can. I love you and I feel blessed to be your father.

G-d — Even though I doubted You at times, I now recognize that everything You have given me has been for my benefit. Thank You for being patient with me and for gifting me the aforementioned people in my life who have helped me realize that. I humbly request from You the strength, wisdom, and resources that will allow me to continue to fulfill my unique mission in this world.

Finally, I would like to thank you, the reader, for taking the time to read my book. I hope that you will find my story not only inspiring, but also relevant and insightful as to how you can handle the adversity in your life.

FOREWORD

URI SCHNEIDER, MA, CCC-SLP; CO-DIRECTOR, SCHNEIDER SPEECH

THE BOOK YOU are holding in your hands is one of a kind. Its unique nature is due to the integrity of its author, and the personal and raw spirit he poured into it. And the degree of its value is as much as you, the reader, choose to make of it. This book, presented through an extraordinarily personal and powerfully vulnerable window, invites you along for an intimate life journey. It is incredibly engaging, inspiring, and it provides a refreshing "lead-by-example" demonstration of how one man faced his life challenge — transcended real adversity with integrity, spirituality, and inarguable success — and how you can too!

I must tell you, when Moe asked me if I would offer a foreword for this book, I was extremely humbled to do so. While I am a professional speech-language pathologist, specializing in stuttering treatment, my knowledge and expertise in the professional sphere are not necessary to the pages of this book. Why not? For this author, Moe Mernick, has become a dear friend and inspiration to me. In this book, Moe retells his story so well that it moved me to tears, and along with many of us who saw the earlier versions of this manuscript, I was invigorated and energized to step up to be better in my personal life.

If you read this book, I am confident you too will share my sentiments and find its value self-evident. So, I deem myself and my professional credentials redundant and out of place.

That being said, what substance and what value can I contribute to this foreword?

I *can* offer some context to stuttering — an enigmatic speech disorder which affects one percent of adults and five percent of children. I have found, notwithstanding its unique characteristics, stuttering has universal qualities which we can all identify with in our own lives. In fact, the experience of dealing with stuttering as part of speech communication is not wholly different from the myriad life challenges each of us face.

(The following ideas are adapted from "Soul-utions in Therapy for People Who Stutter" by Phil and Uri Schneider, in *Stuttering: Inspiring Stories and Professional Wisdom*, StutterTalk Publications, 2012. These ideas offer a soulful frame to understanding stuttering and its treatment — both in terms of the body and the soul aspects of stuttering.)

BODY

Stuttering is a neurological, physical condition that generates unpredictable, involuntary, intermittent interruptions in the automatic, effortless, seamless transition from one sound to the next (or from silence to sound). The frequency and intensity of these interruptions vary widely from moment to moment. We know that it is not simply caused by emotional or cognitive variables. We also know that it is multifactorial and can be exacerbated by any number of triggers, including but not limited to: speech intensity, speech rate, fatigue, emotional arousal, hormonal changes, language complexity, and social-emotional circumstances. The speaker can have a clear flow of thought and motor planning, but can experience interruptions nonetheless.

Consider the typical speech motor system, which can be likened to an intricate ballet performed at super-fast speed (vocal folds the size of your pinky fingernail move hundreds of times per second!). As is true in dance, each articulatory posture in speech needs to transition with flow from the one which precedes it, while, at the same time, preparing for the posture which follows. The physical aspect of stuttering introduces unpredictable disruptions to this intricate ballet, even though the speaker knows "the dance" well and may have performed it tens of thousands of times before without a single glitch. The person who stutters knows what he wants to say and may have, in fact, said the words fluently before. But stuttering is the experience of unintentional interruptions to that regular flow of speech.

There are three different types of disfluencies: hesitations, repetitions, and prolongations. Any person who stutters may have one or more of these disfluencies which characterizes his personal stuttering condition. These terms — hesitations, repetitions, and prolongations — are descriptions of the surface behaviors that are the observable representation of the physical aspect of stuttering. (The traditional assessments use percentage of syllables stuttered

[%SS] as a surface measure of the physical behaviors of stuttering. But these terms and assessments only relate to the physical, "body" aspect of stuttering. When working with a person who stutters, we need to tune in to things that cannot be seen, heard, or measured by outside observation, for the experience which cannot be seen or heard is as real, and possibly even more challenging, than the moment of interrupted speech may be.)

BODY MEETS SOUL

To understand a person's personal human experience with stuttering, one must consider the impact of these physical interruptions on communication and self-image. These unpredictable and undesired physical interruptions can impose upon the speaker's desire to express himself, and reduce his desire to freely connect with others. Over time, this condition can even lead people to avoid speech communication altogether, stifling social, academic, and vocational development and opportunities. If this happens, the person who stutters loses more than his fluency. His soul becomes sore. He may lose faith in the pursuit of his life dreams, which in turn may damage his sense of purpose and sense of self.

Stuttering can make one feel hopelessly and helplessly out of control. When an individual feels robbed of his sense of inner dignity and self-determination, he can develop feelings of shame and humiliation. Interestingly, unlike other speech disorders (like articulation), stuttering can be exacerbated by the increased drive to be heard. It is a fact that if one does not speak, he will not stutter.

Ironically, stuttering affects those who commit to communicating and sharing their inner thoughts, feelings, and ideas with the world!

Peculiarly so, people who stutter usually do not stutter in speech which is not genuine communication.

Now, let's consider how speech communication, stuttering, and speech therapy are really the intersection of metaphysical (soul) elements and physical (body) mechanisms. The physical mechanism of speech communication includes movements, airflow, sounds, words, and grammatical structures. But we must not forget that these physical elements coalesce to serve a special, metaphysical ("soulful") purpose. Universally, speech communication is a means to understanding, which opens the door for compassion, which leads to relationships and connection. Speech communication is the song of soulful communication — a gift endowed to mankind above and beyond all other creatures on this planet. Through our speech communication, we fulfill our inner drive to express our personal thoughts, feelings, needs, and desires, and feel connected to others via a two-way symphony of sound and expression. When we speak out our thoughts and feelings with our voices in exchange with other people, we build bridges of meaning between ourselves, our inner experiences, and others.

Now, if we understand that the experience of being a person who stutters has a "body" and a "soul" aspect to it, then speech therapy and the person's approach in dealing with his issues must also have a body and a soul. The "body" of therapy focuses on the physical mechanics of speech production and the exercises designed to enhance the ease of speech and reduce the frequency and severity of interruptions. This includes the physical training needed to break old behavior patterns and establish new ones. It is significant to note that the physical aspects of therapy have been the primary (sometimes exclusive) focus of our professional tradition, but it is certainly not the only part, and probably not the most meaningful part of the healing process.

In fact, we must also address the underlying, metaphysical "soul" aspects of why we communicate and what we think and feel about our speech, about ourselves as communicators, our self-worth, and most of all, our true purpose in the world. In reality, these soulful elements define the purpose of the work, and they motivate, direct, and drive the efforts required to modify physical mechanisms.

As you'll see in the pages that follow, this soulful approach to therapy was something that Moe discovered on his own. Realizing that his stutter might well be a lifelong condition for him, Moe did not resign himself to it, rather he fully engaged his sense of purpose and meaning. He embraced the idea that he would pursue his dreams and live the happiest and most meaningful life he could, irrespective of whether or not his stutter resolved in therapy or not at all. He had a life worth living — to its fullest. And in an unbelievable twist — not only in spite of his stutter, but because of it!

As you read this book and consider your life's journey, I encourage you to consider the integration of "body" and "soul" — the physical and metaphysical elements — in the process of change. This means that there is more to change than simply learning new skills and techniques. While skills, techniques, treatment, and other physical adjustments are important, one can easily overlook or even dismiss the emotional and spiritual elements that are fundamental to making change possible. Ironically, recognition and acceptance of an issue — identifying how much we can change this issue and how much we cannot — is paramount to the possibility of transcending whatever issue it may be.

As a person who gravitates to documentary films and anything to do with self-improvement, I thoroughly enjoyed and recommend this book for its authentic account of Moe's personal journey of triumph, told through a wonderful read filled with candor and personal examples. I truly hope you find as much inspiration and value in this book as I did.

INTRODUCTION

WHILE I DO not always read mass e-mails (especially those in which the recipient must scroll down past hundreds of other e-mail addresses before actually finding the text), the one dated December 11, 2007, seemed rather unique. Perhaps it was the title that grabbed my attention. Or perhaps it was simply its timing in my inbox, as I was preparing to fly to Central Europe for a large Jewish education program based in the Austrian Alps, and I was on the lookout for good stories to share. Either way, I read the e-mail and was subsequently very happy that I did.

> *A young woman went to her mother and told her about her life and how things were so hard for her. She did not know how she was going to survive it and wanted to give up. She was tired of fighting and struggling. It seemed that as one problem was solved a new one arose.*
>
> *Her mother took her to the kitchen. She filled three pots with water. In the first, she placed carrots, in the second she placed eggs, and in the last she placed ground coffee beans. She let them sit and boil without saying a word.*

In about twenty minutes she turned off the burners. She fished the carrots out and placed them in a bowl. She pulled the eggs out and placed them in a bowl. Then she poured the coffee out into a bowl.

Turning to her daughter, she asked, "Tell me, what do you see?"

"Carrots, eggs, and coffee," her daughter replied.

Her mother brought her closer and asked her to feel the carrots. She did and noted that they were soft. She then asked her daughter to take an egg and break it. After pulling off the shell, she observed the hard-boiled egg. Finally, she asked her daughter to sip the coffee. The daughter smiled as she tasted its rich flavor.

The daughter then asked, "What does it mean, Mother?"

Her mother explained that each of these objects had faced the same adversity — boiling water — but each reacted differently.

The carrot went into the pot strong, hard, and unrelenting. After being subjected to the boiling water, however, it softened and became weak.

The egg had been fragile. Its thin outer shell had protected its liquid interior. But after sitting in the boiling water, its inside became hardened.

The ground coffee beans were unique, however. After they were in the boiling water, they had changed the water.

"Which are you?" she asked her daughter. "When adversity knocks on your door, how do you respond? Are you a carrot, an egg, or a coffee bean?"

I thought to myself, "Which am I?

"Am I the carrot that seems strong, but with pain and adversity, I wilt and become soft and lose my strength?

"Am I the egg that starts with a malleable heart, but changes with the heat? Did I have a flexible spirit, but after death, a breakup, a financial hardship, or some other trial, have I become hardened and stiff? Does my shell look the same, but on the inside am I bitter and tough, with a rigid spirit and a hardened heart?

"Or am I like the coffee bean? The bean actually changes the hot water, the very circumstance that brings the pain. When the water boils the beans, it releases a wonderful aroma and flavor."

If you are like the coffee bean, when things are at their worst, you not only become better, but you change the situation around you to be better.

How do you handle adversity?

Are you a carrot, an egg, or a coffee bean?

CHALLENGES

Since I grew up with a severe stutter, the topic of challenges has always intrigued me. What is their purpose? Where do they truly come from? Is it possible for people today to develop a genuine relationship with G-d, Who actually gives us those very challenges? Ultimately, is it possible to become like the coffee bean (in the above analogy), transforming our challenges into our greatest opportunities?

Growing up as a religious Jew, these questions weighed on me. I was constantly taught that G-d loves us, takes care of us, and always acts in our best interest.

To be honest, though, for much of my life I could not seem to reconcile my stutter with any of that. How could such a loving, caring G-d give me — an innocent, young child — such an embarrassing and inhibiting speech impediment? Things did not add up; it simply did not make any sense.

After much pain and misery, I set out to discover answers to my questions. If He was truly intricately involved with every aspect of my life, I needed to understand how He could make me suffer so much.

SHARING MY JOURNEY

As such, the impetus for this book was not just from the pain, confusion, and embarrassment I felt from my crippling stutter; rather, it was from my journey — learning how to embrace my challenge, grow through it, and gain a deeper relationship with G-d as a result.

Still, even though I was encouraged by speech professionals (and others) to pen my story to inspire others, I didn't fully appreciate the uniqueness of my approach to stuttering (and, on a more fundamental level, all life challenges) — and thus the need for my book — until the following three stories happened to me.

ADVICE TO PARENTS

While I was studying for my MBA (Master of Business Administration), I had a meeting with my career services advisor to discuss various career-related issues. Right before the meeting concluded, my advisor asked for my advice on a personal matter. She and her husband had just discovered that their three-year-old daughter had developed a stutter. Nervous about its long-term implications, they began meeting with speech therapists to see what could be done.

How should they react? What could be done to help their daughter overcome the impediment at an early age?

I advised her as follows:

> As young as your daughter may be, she can pick up on the fact that her parents are extremely worried about her newly-developed speech pattern. As such, she will probably become hesitant to speak, because she won't want to frighten you. It is easier for her to keep her mouth shut and be silent than to watch your panicked facial expressions when she can't seem to get her words out.
>
> The problem with her (very natural) reaction is the "snowball effect." The more she chooses not to speak, the more anxiety she will feel about speaking. Therefore, each time she decides that it is safer not to risk stuttering, she, in effect, is subconsciously developing a mental block against expressing herself verbally. That, of course, should be avoided.
>
> To prevent her from walking on eggshells, you must create a safe environment for her. She must feel that you unconditionally love her and will not be upset or judge her if

she begins to stutter. To do so, you and your husband must become comfortable with the fact that your daughter may stutter for the rest of her life. And it is okay. As you see with me, I hope, people with a stutter can go on to lead productive and rewarding lives.

Know, though, that this process must start with you. The ball is in your court. The more accepting you become, the less your daughter will feel as though you are trying to change her. Then she will feel comfortable to be herself around you, without ever feeling the need to refrain from talking to you.

Ironically, by becoming comfortable with the fact that your daughter may permanently stutter, you are providing her with the best chance of overcoming it. The safe haven of your home will hopefully help her develop strong self-confidence, notwithstanding her speech pattern. You will thereby significantly increase the probability that your daughter's stutter will be but a blip on her early childhood radar screen.

Please note, though, that you cannot expect her to overcome it, as that is, in effect, the opposite of true acceptance of her stutter. She will sense your insincerity and, as a result, that safe haven will not be created. Therefore, I strongly suggest that you and your husband have an important conversation, whereby you recognize the limit of control you have over every aspect of your daughter's life, i.e., her stutter. I am confident that you will see results. Because even if she does not stop stuttering, your relationship with her will no longer be one of deflated hopes and frustration, but rather one of idyllic parental love and unwavering support.

While it was exciting for me to hear that this little girl's stutter eventually faded away, it was even more powerful to receive the feedback that my advice was both novel and refreshing. I was lauded for my "unique" approach to stuttering and was praised for having such a healthy attitude.

"Was it so unique?" I wondered. They had already met with the experts, so why did they feel that my approach was so revolutionary?

ADVICE TO YOUNG ADULTS

One day, I was having dinner with a large group of friends. Feeling empowered to speak freely without being held back by my stutter, I spoke — enough for an acquaintance, who also stuttered, to approach me afterward. The ensuing dialogue, however, was rather unique; what started with him trying to instruct me on how to effectively utilize speech with "targets" (vernacular for methods taught during speech therapy) quickly evolved into a very sad conversation about his stutter.

Until we spoke, I may have only slightly noticed his stutter. He was a nice guy, but our social circles rarely overlapped and, therefore, our conversations were mostly limited to a passing hello. Once he heard how comfortable I had become with my stutter and had seen my newfound conviction to proudly be myself, regardless of my stuttering frequency or display, he was shocked. "Aren't you worried about what people will think?" he asked.

He went on to tell me his tale of woe: He grew up with his father being the rabbi of a congregation. But because he was so nervous about what people might think of him when he stuttered, he did not have the courage to attend his father's synagogue — lest he be called up to the

Torah to recite the blessings! Instead, he attended a different synagogue in town, where he could pray unnoticed, hiding his stutter at all costs.

This guy was in his twenties and still afraid to meet a girl for coffee.

What was even sadder, though, was his vivid admission of his fear of dating. "What happens if the girl finds out that I stutter?!" This guy was in his twenties and still afraid to meet a girl for coffee. My heart went out to him.

He aptly concluded our conversation with a painful analogy describing what it feels like to stutter. "Every moment of every day, it's as though I am walking through a pitch black room, knowing that there is a deep wide hole somewhere in the floor. So each step I take is carefully calculated, as I discern what lies ahead. At all costs, I avoid the risk of getting hurt."

This struck a chord; it sounded agonizingly familiar. This is how I had lived so many years of my life.

But what bothered me even more was that he was so intrigued by my advice that it was almost as though I was preaching a revolutionary approach, when in reality, it was the application of simple, positive psychology. *Why has he never heard this before?* I wondered. *Why haven't his speech therapists convinced him that stuttering doesn't have to be cured?* Indeed, as I had learned, while strategies should be used to whatever extent possible to control one's speech, the way in which one's stutter is framed is significantly more important.

ADVICE TO TEENS

One of my former teachers asked me if I would speak to his fifteen-year-old son, a terrific, well-rounded teenager, whose life was sadly being overtaken by his stutter. Typical of an adolescent with a stutter, he was avoiding various social situations and often exercised "word switching" (more about this in chapter 1) to alleviate the pressure of saying certain seemingly difficult words.

I could relate to what he was going through, felt his pain, and wanted to help. We decided to "meet" by telephone.

We began our first call by spending about twenty minutes on small talk, discussing his hobbies and daily schedule. It was nice to get to know each other before discussing his stutter. Then, after I subtly broached the subject, he shared with me all the information I already knew from his father. I validated his feelings of despair and explained how I could relate to everything he was going through. While we touched on my experiences, the first call was mostly about creating trust and common ground, an invaluable platform for him to gain the confidence to face his stutter head-on.

One week later, on our subsequent call, I worked on building his self-confidence, bringing to his attention some of his wonderful character traits. Then, I assigned him a bit of "homework": "Once a day, do not avoid a social situation because of your stutter." Whether it meant introducing himself to a new student at his school or calling his friend for help with homework, I felt it was necessary for him to stop running from his normal teenage responsibilities and who he truly was.

> *"Once a day, do not avoid a social situation because of your stutter."*

In addition, I included a caveat: When speaking to somebody new, I challenged him to actually be up-front about his stutter, to inform the other party — be it a teacher, new classmate, or friend's parent — that he has a stutter. By doing so relatively early in the conversation, he would circumvent building up anxiety about the typical worry, Oh no, what if I stutter?! He was hesitant, yet up to the challenge.

The next week, he gave me an enthusiastic update. He put himself into new situations and felt great. He sounded as though he was finally breaking out of his shell and feeling happy.

The kicker came about one month later. On his own, he volunteered to deliver a speech in front of the student body of his school (approximately two hundred students). He and his parents were ecstatic; never before did he have the courage to speak publicly like that!

Regardless of how much he stuttered, he confidently stood up to speak. He was not going to allow his stutter to inhibit his ambitions.

He is an example of true courage and success.

DR. MOE? NO.

Each of the parties in the aforementioned stories greatly appreciated my "novel" approach to stuttering. It was as though I had cured them of a rare disease, as if I had a secret potion that created self-confidence. In reality, though, I am neither a speech therapist nor a researcher. I am not a professional and don't claim to have verifiable statistics on what works and what doesn't. (Parenthetically, I am not a writer, either. I am much more comfortable, ironically enough, speaking to a large crowd than putting thoughts to paper. That may explain why much of this book sounds more like a motivational speech than a book.) Rather, I'm just a guy who's determined to lead a meaningful, happy life, and I am unwilling to allow my stutter to prevent that.

As a result of these three stories, however, I realized that my mindset, while not at all revolutionary, it somewhat unique. Being someone who understands the challenge of stuttering, yet is still able to lead a wonderful life, I felt an obligation to share my story with others.

Being someone who understands the challenge of stuttering, yet is still able to lead a wonderful life, I felt an obligation to share my story with others.

Please remember: This book is not a clinical manual on how to stop stuttering; there have been enough of those published that claim to "solve the problem." Some approaches seem to be better than others, while others — which guarantee a cure to what is widely accepted as an incurable impediment — usually do more harm than good.

This book is also not a comprehensive work on the Jewish approach to understanding the age-old question: Why do bad things happen to good people? There are numerous other books that deal exclusively with that important topic, and I highly recommend that you read them. (Please see appendix 5 for a recommended reading list.)

It describes how I changed from a having tangible fear of speaking to delivering motivational speeches worldwide.

This book is different. *The Gift of Stuttering* is my way of sharing my personal story as I learned to embrace my stutter and grow through adversity. It describes how I changed from a having tangible fear of speaking to delivering motivational speeches worldwide. Moreover, what makes the book truly unique is that it opens a window into my spiritual journey, one that helped me create a meaningful relationship with G-d — the One who gave me my challenges in the first place. My thoughts are given over in a way that will help readers, regardless of the particular challenge they are facing, incorporate these valuable insights into their lives.

Ultimately, this is a personal story about my journey to self-acceptance, and finding inner peace and true happiness.

1

WELCOME TO MY LIFE

It was the heart-wrenching realization that the word wasn't coming out of my mouth no matter how hard I tried. I'd stand there, eyes wide, frantically trying to figure out a synonym to use instead. Some other word — any word — that was able to express what I wanted to say while seamlessly placing a Band-Aid over my damaged sentence. The word eventually came, but with a few modifications. It was distorted, as if a magician took out a bouquet of dead withered roses instead of blossoming red ones. No one knew about the clearly thought-out sentence in my head, or that I'd been silently repeating the correct word over and over.

— Madeline Wahl, Associate Editor, Blogs & Community at The Huffington Post

B ORN AND RAISED in Toronto, I almost seemed like an ordinary kid.

My passion for sports drove me to countless Raptors, Blue Jays, and Maple Leafs games, and I joined baseball and ice hockey leagues. As the daredevil in my family, I loved the loopiest and most nauseating rides at Canada's Wonderland, Toronto's local amusement park, and felt like I was truly coming of age when I was finally tall enough for Extreme Skyflyer, a mini bungee-jumping ride.

I disliked school, frequently visited cousins in New York, and loved to snowboard in the winter.

While I may have seemed pretty typical, there was something about me that made me stand out.

I stuttered. A lot.

Unbeknownst to me at the time, I was to remain a member of the one percent.

It began when I was about three years old, at which point my parents were told to ignore it, as most children who begin stuttering before the age of five stop on their own; it is usually just a stage of speech development. Eighty percent of preschool children who begin to stutter grow out of it. The remaining twenty percent — otherwise known as the one percent of the population (approximately three million Americans and seventy million worldwide) — remain with a stutter.[2] Unbeknownst to me at the time, I was to remain a member of the one percent.

---

2   According to the National Stuttering Association (NSA).

HIDING

Some of my earliest memories of my stutter are from the first grade. I vividly remember what it was like when my teacher announced that we would all be called upon to read out loud. Then she systematically began calling on us to read, one by one, moving up and down the rows. Those of you who stutter may understand the dire severity of this situation. My mind would be searching for a solution and invariably would end up with the safest choice: Get out of the room, quick!

"I have to go to the bathroom," I would tell my teacher.

So, there I was, only seven years old, and already strategically mapping out methods on how to avoid embarrassment. Timing was everything, I knew. I had about a five-minute window to go to the bathroom; therefore, my strategy was usually to slip out of class when the second person in front of me began reading. If I timed it correctly, I would slip back into class just after it was my turn. I convinced myself that nobody noticed; and even if they did, it was still far better than the agonizing pain of publicly choking on words that just seemed stuck in my throat.

As a child, hiding from my stuttering was my number one priority. At the beginning of each school year, my parents would explain to my teachers how to minimize circumstances that would require me to speak up. They would ask the teachers not to call on me in class. There were countless times that I had the right answer to a teacher's question, but did not raise my hand due to my fear of stuttering. The praise I would receive for getting the right answer simply was not worth the risk of tripping over my words in the process.

By nature, I felt like an outgoing, spunky kid, but I stifled that part of my personality in many situations. I did not stutter much around my family and close friends, because I was fully comfortable with them.

This is another anomaly about stuttering: it can totally disappear in comfortable, low-anxiety environments.

> This is another anomaly about stuttering: it can totally disappear in comfortable, low-anxiety environments.

Every social situation had to be calculated: Will I have to introduce myself to someone new? What if my friend's parent asks me a question? Am I able to order a slice of pizza without stuttering on the *p*? (Because if not, as much as I loved pizza, I would much prefer to go without the slice.)

RIDICULE

My fear of stuttering was not solely a product of my imagination. Rather, I was subjected to ridicule as a child. When I told my mother that I planned on sharing my experiences in this area, she expressed her excitement, love, and support for the project, recognizing how many people it might help. She then reminisced about the immense challenges that stuttering had introduced into my life.

> But invariably, I would respond (often through tears of hopelessness and despair) that everything was worthless if I couldn't speak — arguably the very thing that makes us human.

She reminded me of one particular time when I returned home from a friend's birthday party in seventh grade and immediately burst into tears. I told her that when I was at the party, a peer of mine had walked by me and mimicked my stuttering right to my face! I was so embarrassed, frustrated, and sad. My mother explained to me, as she lovingly did many times, "Moshe, you are so fortunate; you have so much going for you..." But invariably, I would respond (often through tears of hopelessness and despair) that everything was worthless if I couldn't speak— arguably the very thing that makes us human.

Things were so bad that one of my brothers prayed that he could take part of my stutter from me because of the unbearable pain and heartache he saw me going through, something I only found out about very recently.

WORD SWITCHING

Let us further delve into the world of stuttering.

Perhaps the tool that I have used most often in attempting to prevent stuttering is commonly referred to as "word switching." Naturally, certain words are more difficult to pronounce than others. By that, I do not mean longer versus shorter words. Rather, I am referring specifically to the first consonant of a word and the intensity with which it exits one's lips. For instance, the letter *p* is more abrupt and stronger than the letter *m*, even though they are both formed by using the same contour of the mouth and lips. The letter *p*, it seems, has to burst forth from our lips, whereas the letter *m* can glide out much more easily. (Give it a shot; you'll see for yourself.)

As such, I grew up dwelling on what I was going to say every step of the way. The famous adage "Think about what you say before you say it" holds even truer for those who stutter. When I would think ahead in a sentence I was saying, spot a word that begins with a *p* and feel that I was about to stutter, I would have to scramble to find a synonymous word that would be easier to verbalize. After all, why risk the stutter? This is a wonderful, very popular method used by those who stutter; one I use to this very day.[3]

This technique, however, is not perfect. It becomes much more challenging when there is a specific text from which one must read. It is for this reason, as I am sure you can imagine, that I avoided reading in class. After all, everyone had the same text in front of them. If I were to switch a harder-sounding word for an easier-sounding word, my teacher and my classmates would know that I didn't read the text correctly.

Also, word switching is of no use with words that must be spoken. For instance, the first three digits of my home phone number when I was growing up were 6-3-3. For whatever reason, my mind decided that "six" was relatively easy to say, while "three" was not. Thus, because it was necessary for me to say "three" (there was no way to relay my number to someone without enunciating it), the anxiety I felt about this number only increased.

As a result, saying my own telephone number was extremely challenging. If I remember correctly, to circumvent the issue of saying the number "three" when I was young, I even used simple mathematics to help me out, i.e., "My number is 6-(2+1)-(2+1)..."

---

[3] While writing this section of the book, I recalled a recent dinner I had with my family. I was reading a story, word for word, to all those present at the table. At one point, I spotted a word that my brain instantly disliked, so I swapped it for a more pronounceable synonymous word. No one even knew that this took place.

MOSHE = MOE

Similarly, I question to this day whether my switch from the name Moshe to Moe in ninth grade was — at least partially — an anti-stuttering tactic. As previously discussed, the letter *m* is smooth (and therefore relatively easy) to pronounce. Still, I had stuttered countless times saying my name (because one can't just switch one's name!), and I associated the name Moshe with stuttering.

"What's your name?" is one of the most common questions we are asked in our lifetime and I was therefore scarred from all those times I simply could not respond with one simple word, "Moshe."

Moe just seemed easier. It also sounded cooler, at least to me, when I was in ninth grade. It had one syllable, not two; it connoted a fresh start. It almost felt like I was taking on a new persona when being asked for my name; I was no longer the Moshe who stuttered for so many years. Instead, my name was Moe, I was fourteen years old, and I was just like everyone else. Well, at least I wanted to be.

I was no longer the Moshe who stuttered for so many years; instead, my name was Moe.

Sadly, this is not a joke. This is frequently the world of a stutterer: the painstaking inability to express one's name and telephone number.

OH NO, NOT "HELLO"!

In a similar vein, what word is a part of nearly every phone call? What word begins a conversation, without which things don't even get off the ground?

"Hello."

Welcome to My Life

At one point, my brain decided that it was too difficult to say this word. The anxiety of being incapable of switching the "hello" for any other word spiraled into a completely irrational determination that "hello" could not be expressed without stuttering.

And so it was. As bizarre as it may seem, there were times when I was simply unable to enunciate the word "hello." I was about eight years old when this occurred, and I still remember the feelings of helplessness and utter hopelessness when I picked up the phone and couldn't even initiate the conversation with that one simple five-letter word.

I would stand nearby, usually with tears in my eyes, thinking that there wasn't anything wrong with our phone; instead, there was something wrong with me. Why couldn't I say the word "hello"?

Those who had called my house repeatedly said, "Hello, hello, hello... Anyone there?" And there I was on the other end of the line, turning shades of red and purple that I never knew existed, unable to enunciate a sound. Sometimes people called back to inform my mother that there must be something wrong with our phone. I would stand nearby, usually with tears in my eyes, thinking that there wasn't anything wrong with our phone; instead, there was something wrong with me. Why couldn't I say the word "hello"?

I was miserable. What would life have in store for me? How would I ever finish high school or pass a job interview? Which girl would want to marry me? What would I sound like when reading bedtime stories to my kids?

My pain and fear ran deep.

SYNAGOGUE CHALLENGES

This issue often arose in the setting of the synagogue as well. When a Jewish boy celebrates his bar mitzvah (at thirteen years old), he is typically called upon in the synagogue to recite a blessing in front of the entire congregation. Subsequently, from the age of thirteen and on, this opportunity arises regularly — and even more often for a *Kohein*[4] like myself. The Torah is read three times a week. In essence, three days did not go by without my being afraid that I would be called upon to recite these blessings in front of the congregation.

The *Birchat Kohanim* ritual[5] was a challenge too. Blessing the entire congregation should have felt like a privilege; it should have been the highlight of my times in the synagogue. But in reality, it was just another aspect of Judaism that posed a challenge due to my stutter.

Not only do I recall the fear of being spontaneously called up to the Torah or to perform *Birchat Kohanim*, but I also dreaded being in a situation where I could not swap words. The blessings were short, simple, and in Hebrew. Thus, with no way to employ my word-switching tactic, being called upon was one of my worst nightmares.

While I am not proud of the following, I suspect that I'm far from being the only Jewish teenager (who stutters) to react this way:

I used to either intentionally skip synagogue services on Torah-reading days, or, if I did attend, I would make it a habit to slip out "to

---

4   In Judaism, *Kohanim* (singular: *Kohein*) are the priestly class who perform certain ceremonial functions.

5   *Birchat Kohanim*, or the Priestly Blessing, is a ritual performed outside of Israel during prayer services on the major festivals, where all of the *Kohanim* in attendance ascend the podium and, in unison, pronounce a special blessing over the rest of the congregation. In Israel, this ritual is performed during prayer services every day of the year.

the bathroom" right around the window of time when I would be called upon. As you can see, not much changed from when I was a youngster to when I grew into my teens — only an increased amount of insecurity and anxiety revolving around my speaking abilities and the hundreds of hours I had spent in speech therapy.

SPEECH THERAPY

To put it mildly, I found my stutter to be extremely distasteful. Therefore, my parents and I invested enormous of amounts of time, energy, and resources into speech therapy. We were willing to do anything possible to put an end to it.

Reflecting back on my earlier years, I remember visiting several speech therapists, but for one reason or another, none of them worked for me. In order to be successful, it needed to "click," and none of them seemed to be the right match.

Many speech therapists make one of the following two mistakes:

- Laser-focusing on the clinical aspect of stuttering, they don't focus on the emotional toll that stuttering takes — including the inevitable negative effect it has on one's self-esteem.
- Actively seeking to "cure" their patients of their impediment, they don't adequately impart the message that they can only equip their clients with tools to help control their stutter, not completely get rid of it.

Also, to illustrate the possibility of leading a productive life, speech therapists often tout a long list of famous people who stuttered, including Winston Churchill, King George VI of England, Marilyn Monroe, Elvis Presley, Tiger Woods, and Jack Welch (see appendix 3 for a more comprehensive list). But that never made me feel much better. First of all, none of those celebrities seemed even remotely relatable. And second of all, because most of them didn't stutter anymore, it was as if they were hinting that I, too, could overcome my stutter. And while that may have provided me with a temporary high, it carried with it the very real risk of setting me up for disappointment when my stutter continued — as is usually the case with adolescent and adult stutterers.

Weren't these "professional" speech therapists aware of the NSA's famous survey on stuttering, in which they received responses from 1,235 people, including 686 adults and 31 teens who stutter? One of the key conclusions was: Changing one's attitude toward speaking and stuttering was the most successful therapy approach for both children and adults.

Why, therefore, was there such an obsession about curing the stutter and less of a focus on self-acceptance? At the very least, a healthy combination of the two would have sufficed.

Granted, even though I was disenchanted with numerous speech therapists and therapeutic approaches, I was appreciative that I wasn't seeing them fifty years ago. Israeli-born Professor Ehud Yairi, an international expert on stuttering who currently resides in the United States, describes the treatments he received when he was growing up, which seem rather bizarre:

> At the time, there were a small number of doctors who had an interest in stuttering, and there were no communication

Welcome to My Life

therapists. One doctor told me to put my feet in a bucket of cold water every evening for fifteen minutes. Another suggested sitting next to the window, looking out at the greenery, and breathing in the good wind and letting out the bad wind. They told me to read passages from the newspaper aloud and...to talk along with a metronome. I received electric shocks to my face and neck muscles, I was injected with sodium pentothal that was supposed to reach my subconscious, I moved my right thumb from side to side, I practiced breathing, someone gave me an injection in the behind that was supposed to calm me. They worked on me with hypnosis; for two years I was in psychoanalysis. Everything was a total waste of time.

THEN I MET LAURA

My attitude toward speech therapy changed when I met Laura. She was young; she was fun. But most importantly, she treated me with respect. Laura also ran her speech therapy practice out of her living room, which definitely added to a homier, warmer, and less clinical ambience.

My hour-long appointments were actually enjoyable. They usually consisted of working through certain techniques that, if used correctly, could ultimately help me gain more control over my speech. Some of the techniques (or "targets") included:

Full Breath — A deep breath before speaking, which helps ensure that there is enough gusto to last long enough to express one's thought.

Easy Onset — Lightly beginning the first letter in a word, which enables one to more easily slide into the sound without getting "blocked."

Full Contour — Once the first sound is out, blending the words enables one to smoothly ride out the words between breaths.

Afterward, I would skim through a phone book and begin calling random stores to ask them questions. For instance, I would say, "Hi, my name is Moshe. Until what time are you open today? Thank you very much."

When I was having a particularly challenging time saying certain words or letters, Laura would encourage me to focus on those in my calls. For instance, if I had a hard time saying the number "three" (as discussed earlier in this chapter), I would call stores and restaurants (with written questions in front of me, so I wouldn't be able to "word switch") and ask the following types of questions:

"Hi, are you open past three o'clock today?"

"Do you have more than three locations in Toronto?"

"Can you please name three options on your lunch menu?"

As odd as it may sound, making these calls was actually fun. After all, as I sat there feeling secure with Laura by my side, I was actually able to speak to others fluently. It felt magical; Laura's living room had become my oasis of fluency — what I considered normalcy to be like.

A huge burden had been lifted — as temporary as those calls may have been — bringing me much satisfaction and boosting my self-esteem. Finally.

Even the homework was tolerable.

Oftentimes, it only consisted of me making dozens of similar phone calls, and either recording the call or jotting down the results.

But the most exciting part of my time with Laura was when we moved on to doing "transfers." This meant that instead of sitting in her living room making phone calls or reviewing methods to improve fluency, I would actually go with her to a nearby coffee shop or shopping mall to practice face-to-face encounters, which obviously were much more anxiety-ridden than phone calls. (As daunting as it was, though, it was great to leave school in the middle of the day to walk around a shopping mall without getting in trouble for it!) Once again, Laura would encourage me to focus on the areas in which I was struggling, allowing me to slowly build the self-confidence which would, one day, enable me to function regularly in social settings by not hiding behind my stutter.

My friends must have thought I had serious health issues. Every other week or so, throughout my elementary school career, I would leave school for nearly two hours, simply stating that I had a doctor's appointment. It must have sounded a little strange — perhaps even more suspicious and strange than had I just been open with them and simply told them that I was going to my speech therapist. But this was all part of the disguise I tried to wear throughout my childhood; I neither wanted to admit to my stutter, nor did I wish to draw any attention to it. I just wished and often pretended that it did not exist.

I just wanted to be a "normal" kid.

BAR MITZVAH ANXIETY

After my twelfth birthday, it dawned on me that my bar mitzvah was fast approaching. And while that may have been an exciting time for most of my classmates, it actually petrified me. Not only would I have to read from the Torah in front of the entire synagogue, but I would also be expected to give a speech! These were things that I not only had never done before, but actually dreaded. How was I going to face several hundred people with my tongue flailing and face jerking uncontrollably?

Laura came to the rescue. We spent many months reviewing my bar mitzvah speech, word for word, and focusing on the blessings I would be saying over the Torah. It occurred to me how bizarre this entire episode was. While my friends and other "regular" twelve year olds, were discussing what kinds of presents they would be receiving, I was panic-stricken about saying a few words in public. Yes, my friends also had to practice for their speeches. But why did I have to spend dozens, if not hundreds, of hours practicing for this one speech?

It was around this time that my sadness and confusion began to surface, turning into anger.

ANGRY WITH G-D

I did not like the stuttering at all. Where did it come from?

Why me?

Having grown up in an observant Jewish home and attending Jewish schools, I had been inculcated with the understanding that there is a G-d who created the world and controls all that is within it. He not only looks at the world from on high, but He is intimately involved with everything that goes on here on Earth, including every aspect of my life. I was also taught that His love for me was beyond anything I could imagine and that everything that happens is for my benefit.

But for me, a teenager-to-be, my life seemed void of a Creator. After all, if G-d was, like all my teachers said He was, an all-loving Father, why would He make me go through so much pain? It had already been so many years that I had a stutter, and the future wasn't looking promising. What did I do wrong? Did I deserve this?

> But for me, a teenager-to-be, my life seemed void of a Creator.

Finally, if He had the power to give me a stutter, why wouldn't He just take it away?! These seemingly unanswerable questions were beginning to chip away at me incessantly, eroding the very foundation upon which my religious upbringing was based. And as a result, my relationship with G-d (and Judaism, for that matter) was being called into question.

2

GROWING PAINS

The major part is really underneath the surface. That is, the person feels fear, shame, guilt, tension. He's always worried about what might happen — he might get into a situation and not be able to say his name, or the telephone rings and he can't answer it.

And in this way, stuttering is like an iceberg: The part that you see is really the smaller part; the larger part, to the stutterer, is all the emotional load he has to carry along with him at all times.

— "The Way We Talk," Documentary on Stuttering (2014)

I HAD MIRACULOUSLY DELIVERED my bar mitzvah speech fluently, putting me (and those around me) on a temporary high. It offered me a glimmer of hope that maybe — just maybe — I would be able to speak like that more often.

"One day," I hoped.

However, I doubted myself: Indeed, my speech went well, but perhaps that was just because I invested hundreds of hours practicing it, word by word. Would that method be practical on any level for the future?

What about dating? What about job interviews? And if Laura would not be sitting there in the front row cheering me on, how would I be able to I express myself without my stutter getting in the way?

> *My downward spiral had begun.*

The above erosion of self-confidence began to take hold. Insecurities revolving around my stutter only increased, and as I watched the clock continue to tick into my teenage years, I was saddened and frustrated that my stutter had not yet taken leave.

My downward spiral had begun.

REBELLION

I was facing a very challenging road ahead. Not only was my stutter in full force at an age where social acceptance was of primary importance, but my parents were also in the early stages of a complicated, difficult divorce.

> *I simply could not reconcile the philosophical disconnect between my adversity and the concept of an all-loving G-d that I had been taught.*

I simply could not reconcile the philosophical disconnect between my adversity and the concept of an all-loving G-d that I had been taught. Granted, He might be in control of the world. But does He even know that I exist? Does He even care about me? And if so, the extremely challenging circumstances in my life didn't seem to make any sense!

So I rebelled, mostly in subtle ways, against the religious lifestyle in which I had been raised and the path on which I was expected to traverse. I needed some time to explore the world around me, to discover clarity amidst my pain and confusion.

One way that I rebelled was by pursuing an acting career, something that did not exactly jive with my religious upbringing. Immaturely, I dreamed that the fame and fortune that comes with a Hollywood lifestyle would overshadow anything I was struggling with, and would somehow fill the void created by my anger at G-d.

I must say, He has a fantastic sense of humor.

After I finally convinced my mother to sign the waiver at the talent agency (necessary for kids under the age of sixteen), I was called for my first role as an extra — I was to play the part of a Chassidic Jew! So just as I was using this acting tool to inch away from my level of observance, G-d made me look even more observant!

> *I was to play the part of a Chassidic Jew!*

My short-lived acting career went on to include appearances as an extra in films and TV shows with numerous big-name celebrities. While it was a fun, adventurous ride (that helped me pocket some spending money), I decided that becoming a Hollywood star was not the track I truly wanted for myself. Many people I met lacked depth and refinement, character traits I took for granted in my community. Moreover, it became clear to me that becoming a successful actor would significantly increase the probability of my living a dysfunctional life, and I did not want to risk one of my most important goals in life — raising a healthy, happy family. Somehow, deep down, I felt that taking shape as a priority in my life.

Reflecting back, it is interesting to discern to what degree my stutter influenced that decision. If I had fluent speech, would I have jumped into acting classes at a younger age? Would I have asked my agent to send me on auditions for speaking roles? It was easy to be a film extra because it completely circumvented the necessity to speak in front of the camera. What about speaking roles, though? Why did I not pursue them more? Did my fear of stuttering consciously play a role in those decisions?

It recently occurred to me that whatever held me back from pursuing a full acting career, be it stuttering or something else, it was truly a blessing in disguise. I am appreciative with the way my life has taken shape, and I am therefore extremely grateful that I did not venture further down that path.

HIGH SCHOOL DRAMA

It is debatable whether my ensuing high school career, or lack thereof, was due to my inability to comprehend the age-old philosophical conundrum of challenges, sheer rebelliousness, or some combination of the two. Regardless, it was a bumpy ride.

At the age of fifteen and midway through the tenth grade, I had already attended three different yeshiva high schools in three different cities.

At the age of fifteen and midway through the tenth grade, I had already attended three different yeshiva high schools in three different cities. Clearly, the conventional track was not working for me. Not only did I require more individual attention, but I also needed an environment where I could search for deep, relevant answers to my questions. As I mentioned earlier, I felt that I wanted to penetrate the depths of truth in order to reach a decision on where and how I would lead my life. My feelings called into question whether G-d really loved me, something I had always been taught in my religious upbringing. If this was not the case, then I would reevaluate my spiritual direction in life.

Reflecting back, at some level I always knew that G-d was there with me. I just couldn't fathom how that could be. I vividly remember being upset with Him and expressing it. It wasn't that I doubted the fact that He created and runs the world; rather, the spiritual disconnect was on a more personal level. Why did I have to stutter so much for so long? What was happening with my countless, heartfelt prayers? Finally, how could He add such a difficult layer of adversity (i.e., my parents' divorce) on top of my stutter?

Frankly, because I did not feel that I had the strength or resources to adequately deal with my challenges, I was angry at G-d for giving me them in the first place.

OFF TO ISRAEL

An alternative high school program, nestled in Israel's isolated northern city of Tzfat (Safed), seemed to be the right choice for me — as strange as that may sound for a fifteen year old from Toronto. By living six thousand miles away from home in a country I was to quickly come to cherish and appreciate, I was able to leverage my independence, time, and space into a unique opportunity to reflect on my past and think about my future.

(Please note: I normally do not recommend that fifteen year olds attend high school thousands of miles from home. My unique circumstances, however, necessitated that choice.)

Geared for North American teenagers, this program combined extreme outdoor activities with enriched informal education classes on Judaism (and, of course, different tracks to complete high school). For the first time in my life, I went on an intense two-day mountain biking trip, camped out for several days at the Dead Sea, and went scuba diving off the coast of Eilat.

Moreover, Torah study took on an entirely different meaning. I began to learn because I wanted to, not because I had to. I delved into topics that intrigued me, rather than a predefined curriculum that seemed irrelevant to me.

I had deeply connected with the works of Rabbi Moshe Chaim Luzzatto, a brilliant fifteenth-century author and kabbalist (otherwise known by his acronym, Ramchal). I had a special one-on-one study session with Rabbi Eliyahu Reiter, a guitarist for the renowned band, Simply Tzfat. He was able to delve into the depth of the Ramchal's writings and make them relevant to my stage in life. And so great had our love been for the Ramchal's teachings that Rabbi Reiter and I even prayed together at his burial site in Tiveria (Tiberias) on the anniversary of his death, at sunrise. It was a powerful early morning experience.

Fascinatingly, the Ramchal lays out the purpose of the world right at the beginning of *Mesillat Yesharim* (*The Path of the Just*), one of his popular works. He states categorically that in order to properly live in this world, we must first understand our purpose — why it is that we were created in the first place.

This notion, by the way, is not exclusively Jewish. In his highly acclaimed bestselling book, *How to Win Friends and Influence People*, Dale Carnegie echoes a similar sentiment, albeit at a much simpler level. He provides his readers with clear, practical advice: Begin with the end in mind. By being clear about our goals, he explains, we are well on our way to achieving success. We not only become far less distracted, but we also become significantly more focused. Each and every day becomes infused with mission and purpose. How many of us flippantly move through life, bouncing from one experience to the next without having a clear picture of what we would like to truly accomplish?

While this advice is mostly geared toward gaining clarity on traditional goals, such as family, career, and community involvement, it also can be extended to something far more fundamental: What is one's purpose in the world?

I learned later in my career (as a strategy consultant for Deloitte in business development for several high-tech startups) that every company also needs a clearly defined vision. They will even spend excessive time and money to clarify it.

Why? Because when trying to interest investors in their company, they must present a crystallized business plan that clearly defines their roadmap. The most important element in it is their ultimate goal. In which consumer segments and geographies do they envision their penetration? For startups, do they seek an IPO (initial public offering) or an acquisition, and how does that affect their immediate strategy?

Working toward a goal is a useful objective in every area of life. Another example of this is raising children, in that we choose schools and communities that reflect the values and education we hope to inculcate in them.

Yet another practical example is our jobs. If we are hired to work on a project, but we are not exactly sure what the end result should look like, it is difficult to even get started. Imagine a construction worker building a condominium without every iota of the plans mapped out in clear detail!

Of course, the Ramchal had it right. Because when it comes to spirituality, more than anything else, we must first understand the framework of the world around us, and only then can we understand the context, mission, and purpose of our lives.

While I did not yet understand my life's mission, I knew — for the first time in my life — that I was finally on my way to discovering it.

TERROR IN ISRAEL

One August afternoon, my friend and I met for lunch at Big Apple Pizza in the heart of Jerusalem. Afterward, we tried to hail a taxi to go across town, but the taxis were all full. Finally, we were motioned to by a taxi driver across the street, headed in the opposite direction. I hesitated though. This driver would have to go all the way around the crowded streets to arrive at my destination and would probably charge us extra for the trip. Was it worth it to go with him or should we wait for another cab going in my direction?

I opted for the cab, and the driver alleviated my concern by attempting a U-turn, albeit unsuccessfully. The streets were simply too crowded, so we began to circle the block.

I then heard what has been, to this very day, one of the eeriest sounds I have ever heard: *BOOM!*

The sound was unlike any other, a sound I had never before heard in Toronto. *What could it be?* I wondered.

A tear welled up in my eye as I suspected the worst. My taxi driver shrugged it off; sounds like that may have seemed normal to him. Moments later, however, my worst suspicions were confirmed as numerous ambulances and media personnel rushed right past us.

I hadn't realized how close I had been to the suicide bombing until my taxi driver turned on the all-Hebrew radio station and, after hearing the details of what took place, exclaimed, *"We were right there!" "We were right there!"*

The story was later clarified to me: Several stores down from where I had caught the cab, a young female terrorist entered Sbarro, a popular, crowded pizza store in the center of Jerusalem, and blew herself up. Fifteen civilians — including seven children and a pregnant woman — were killed, while another hundred and thirty people were wounded.

My heart was broken and my body felt paralyzed — not only for all those affected, but also because of my near encounter with death. What would have happened had I waited another few minutes to hail a taxi going in the right direction? Even worse, what would have happened had I hailed a taxi going in the right direction…and been right in front of Sbarro when the terrorist blew herself up?

DID I JUST KILL ADAM?

Approximately thirty minutes before the explosion, I had bumped into Adam, someone I knew from Toronto. He was lost. While I could not tell him exactly how to get to his destination, I thought I would send him to the popular intersection nearby, where he would find many Americans and Israelis who could give him better directions.

"Go to the intersection of Yafo Street and King George," I suggested. "You'll see Sbarro, a big pizza store, and I'm sure people there will be better able to direct you."

After gaining my bearings later that day, I couldn't stop thinking about Adam. Where was he when the attack took place? Was he okay? What did I do?

After what seemed like an eternity, word came back that Adam was fine. But it wasn't until a few days later that I had the chance to hear his story firsthand.

"Adam, I thought I might have killed you!" I exclaimed upon first seeing him.

"You almost did!" was his initial response. He then proceeded to describe the chain of events that took place after we left off.

"Taking your suggestion to head to Yafo Street and King George, I leisurely strolled over, window shopping along the way. Then, as I eyed the intersection you told me about, I decided I would first get some lunch at Sbarro. When I was almost there, it happened...the store blew up right in front me! I saw body parts fly over my head and had other people's blood splattered on my sandals. I was freaked out and began to run. But then I came back to help those who were injured."

"Moe," Adam continued, "had the store blown up thirty seconds later, I would have been the one flying over other people's heads."

APPRECIATING LIFE

With the sound of the blast fresh in my mind, I was feeling, perhaps for the first time, appreciative of my lot in life.

Life took on a meaning that it never had before. It was no longer about the pizza I had for lunch, the entertainment I had scheduled for the afternoon, and my disappointment in my inability to speak like everyone else. With the sound of the blast fresh in my

56   THE GIFT OF STUTTERING

mind, I was feeling, perhaps for the first time, appreciative of my lot in life. I was feeling appreciative that I had chosen Big Apple Pizza rather than choosing Sbarro; I was feeling appreciative that my taxi driver was unable to make his U-turn; and I was feeling appreciative that Adam had delayed his lunch by deciding to window-shop along the way.

At that moment, my stutter seemed somewhat insignificant in the scheme of things. I was simply appreciative to live another day.

NEW ROLE MODEL

But perhaps the most fascinating and memorable part of my time in Tzfat was getting to know Ari Bensoussan. Originally from Brooklyn, New York, Ari was one of the leaders of the program I attended. He was outgoing, funny, and personable. He was also a sensational speaker, and often had me and the other participants laughing hysterically at his inspirational stories.

Oh, and also, Ari had a (fairly severe) stutter.

It did not make any sense to me at the time. When speaking to Ari one-on-one, he would stutter regularly, just like other stutterers I had met. When he stood up to speak in front of a crowd, however, he never stuttered! His speech was calculated; his voice was dramatic; his passion was palpable.

There were famous people who stuttered, such as Winston Churchill and Marilynn Monroe, who were known for their oratory skills too. But I had never met someone with a stutter who was able to execute a speech like that. How did Ari Bensoussan do it? What was his secret?

As much as I admired his confident and fluent public speaking, what struck me even more was his positive go-getter attitude toward life. He stuttered. Badly. It must have been embarrassing for many years. How did he manage to always walk around with a smile? More importantly, what gave him the inner strength to overcome the attendant self-pity and to become so socially adept — to help run a summer program, teach classes, enthusiastically meet new people, and have a positive attitude toward dating? How did he do it?

> He stuttered. Badly. It must have been embarrassing for many years. How did he manage to always walk around with a smile?

Again, I couldn't help but wonder, *What was his secret?*

Later, I discovered that Ari had gone through another major challenge in life: cancer. When he was eighteen years old, he underwent chemotherapy for the first time, and the radiation caused him to lose all of his hair. Nevertheless, he somehow managed to maintain his positive attitude.

Ari was a superstar. It occurred to me that Ari's positivity and focus in life were not haphazard; it could not simply be a coincidence. Rather, he must have grown through his challenges. He must have reflected on the struggles in his life and made a conscious effort to become an incredible person — not despite his challenges, but because of them.

> He must have reflected on the struggles in his life and made a conscious effort to become an incredible person — not despite his challenges, but because of them.

Every day was a gift. His ability to speak publicly, albeit with a speech impediment, was a gift. It became increasingly clear to me that his passionate, inspiring teaching style was a result of his personal growth. Everyone felt his sincerity, his love, his genuine appreciation for life.

It does not surprise me at all that today Ari is a popular rabbi, a wonderful husband, and a loving father.

Ari was my role model. In my own distinctive way, I too wanted to prevail over my stutter. Yet more than my burning desire to speak with fluency, I was eager to break loose of the baggage that came along with my stutter — namely my social avoidance, low self-confidence, and dispassionate relationship with G-d.

I wanted to stop feeling sorry for myself; I wanted to be happier. But how? What was Ari's secret?

3

LEARNING TO DEAL WITH CHALLENGES

Understanding is the first step to acceptance,
and only with acceptance can there be recovery.

— Albus Dumbledore

MY TIME IN Tzfat was both productive and enjoyable, and it allowed me some much-needed time and space. That summer, though, I was faced with a big decision.

Would I go back to Toronto to complete high school in either a community Jewish high school or public school, or remain in Israel to do the same? I was still fifteen. But I quickly realized that "age is but a number"; I felt many years my senior due to all my life experience. I therefore felt uncomfortable returning to Toronto for a number of reasons.

Insofar as I had already gained much independence and maturity during my time spent abroad, I was leaning toward staying in Israel and fast-tracking through high school. Furthermore, it was important to me to be able to continue exploring my theological questions, and for that, Israel seemed significantly more conducive. Lastly, the situation at home was still tense; hence, maintaining my independence abroad seemed like the healthier choice. The decision to stay in Israel, therefore, seemed pretty clear.

Nevertheless, I still didn't feel entirely comfortable staying in Tzfat. While the program was initially terrific for me, some participants were struggling with serious issues and I badly wanted to join a more established yeshiva, both for the rigor of the learning and for the mainstream integration.

But where would I go? Who would accept me? As a fifteen-year-old who should have been starting eleventh grade, I didn't feel too optimistic about my prospects. Still, with the support and encouragement from my parents, teachers, and mentors, I was determined to give it a shot.

A friend of mine from Tzfat, who had left for a yeshiva in Jerusalem, connected me with Derech, a post-high school program at Ohr Somayach, a large yeshiva in Jerusalem. He described my background to the *rosh yeshiva* (dean), and he was willing to interview me. Enthusiastic about that possibility, I traveled to Jerusalem for the meeting.

And then I had a strange feeling. For one of the first times in my life, I felt a strong need to pray, to pour out my heart to

> For one of the first times in my life, I felt a strong need to pray, to pour out my heart to G-d, asking Him for help.

G-d, asking Him for help. After all, my yearning to attend a yeshiva rather than a public school was mainly to further explore meaning and purpose in the world, and my relationship with my Creator. Stuttering notwithstanding, my anger had somewhat subsided and I was now on a search for understanding.

After all, I felt, *wouldn't He want to help me find the right place where I could do this?*

THE WALL

One of the distinct advantages of being in Israel, or especially in Jerusalem, is the close proximity to the *Kotel* (Western Wall). As the last standing vestige of the retaining wall around the Second Temple that was destroyed approximately two thousand years ago, the *Kotel* remains the holiest place in the world for Jews — and the most apropos and popular location for a heartfelt prayer.

Walking through the winding, cobblestone streets of the Old City, I felt that this visit would be a memorable one. The *Kotel* was not going to be just another tourist attraction for me, where I would take a picture and check it off my list of places to visit; rather, it was going to be a vehicle to connect me to G-d in a more powerful way than ever before. Throughout my life, especially due to my struggles with fluency, I had never really stopped talking to G-d; but our conversation, especially of late, was full of my expressions of confusion, rather than heartfelt requests and openness to connection.

As I descended the stone stairway, with the Kotel *in sight, all my feelings of loneliness and confusion began bubbling to the surface, and as soon as I reached the* Kotel, *I couldn't hold it in any longer.*

As I descended the stone stairway, with the *Kotel* in sight, all my feelings of loneliness and confusion began bubbling to the surface, and as soon as I reached the *Kotel*, I couldn't hold it in any longer.

I burst out crying. Tears streamed uncontrollably down my cheeks. Words were indiscernible, as I couldn't stop bawling.

> *How did I get here in the first place? I am only fifteen years old. I feel so lost, so lonely, so confused. My challenges seem almost insurmountable. It has been so hard to understand why You have given me such difficult challenges, such as my stutter.*
>
> *I reacted to my problems by rebelling and distancing myself from You. But I want to come back. I really do. I want to rebuild a relationship with You. I want to better understand You. And I want to better understand my purpose.*
>
> *I am only fifteen years old. I have no one to truly vouch for me. I am six thousand miles away from my family, and trying to get accepted into a mainstream yeshiva. This would not normally be possible. But deep down, I know that You can help. You can do anything, apparently. Please do so. I am doing this for You. I know that You want me to become closer to You, and for the first time in my life, I am begging You to help me do so.*

The tears continued to flow. It was perhaps the greatest and most genuine crying episode of my adolescence. My emotions had been so pent up, and here, with the perfect outlet, I was finally able to channel them into heartfelt prayer.

It felt so good to feel connected again.

Then, as if out of nowhere, an elderly

> It felt so good to feel connected again.

Learning to Deal with Challenges 63

gentleman approached me and warmly commented, "Everything is going to be okay."

Whether it was Eliyahu HaNavi (Elijah the Prophet) or not, I definitely took it as a sign from G-d, a wink from Heaven, that He heard me and was going to take care of me.

YESHIVA

My interview at Ohr Somayach was off to a great start. I was able to confidently explain who I was, where I wanted to go, and how Ohr Somayach would help me get there. At the end of what seemed to be a positive discussion, however, the rabbi's tone of voice somewhat changed.

"Moe, I heard that you are only sixteen."

Oh no, the dreaded question about my age...

I had conveniently used my Hebrew birthday, perhaps for the first time since my bar mitzvah, because it fell some time before my English birthday that year. To pitch myself as a sixteen-year-old was better than being a fifteen-year-old. Nevertheless, sixteen was still young for a post-high school program.

"When will you be seventeen?"

The spotlight was on me. Until that defining question, all the cards seemed to be lining up for me to be accepted. The rabbi's only hesitation, clearly, was that I would be at least two years younger than the rest of the students. Judaism values honesty, but in certain rare extenuating circumstances, there are exceptions. Is this a circumstance in which G-d would want me to bend the truth?

No way. Honesty is of paramount importance. And if the yeshiva were to decide not to accept me due to a factor beyond my control (i.e., my age), then clearly it was not the right place for me.

"Rabbi," I began, breaking into a big smile, "it's going to be a while."

There it was — out in the open. The one hundred percent truth. It felt as though I had just stepped off a cliff and was waiting for G-d to catch me.

The rabbi smiled right back at me and said, "The truth; I like that." He passed an application form to me.

> *The rabbi smiled right back at me and said, "The truth; I like that."*

I was in! I got accepted into the first yeshiva I applied to, right after pouring out my heart to G-d like I had never done before. It felt so good to know that He had been listening to my prayers all along, even though the answer had not always been yes.

It simply felt so right to take that big next step to Ohr Somayach.

SPIRITUAL GROWTH

The Torah learning was idyllic, because I was soaking up beautiful, deep, and relevant Torah insights from world-renowned rabbis. I could not ask for a better setup.

I took advantage of my surroundings by not only attending numerous lectures and honing my Gemara (Talmud) skills, but I also spent quality time delving into the topics that interested me most, namely prayer and dealing with life challenges. After all, it was primarily my stutter that had brought me to this point; it seemed that the next natural step should be to face my struggles head-on.

In doing so, I wanted to delve even further into the concept from Ramchal that I had begun to learn in Tzfat — the question that had long gnawed away at me, namely, if G-d wanted us to derive ultimate pleasure, and that pleasure was to be truly experienced in the World to Come, why bring mankind to this earthly existence in the first place? Wouldn't it be simpler to be born into an oasis of pleasure, without the challenges that first face us here in this world?

It was as simple as that. Granted, G-d wants to give us pleasure. And granted, that would only fully manifest in the World to Come. But there still seemed to be too much pain on personal (i.e., my stuttering) and national (i.e., war) levels to validate the elongated stopover on the planet Earth. Is it really necessary?

An analogy, which I formulated over time with the help of my rabbis, helps clarify the answer. I will simplify it as follows:

> *Take, for example, a recent college graduate hoping to take a road trip with his friends across America. It is destined to be the trip of a lifetime. The detailed itinerary is planned, from Los Angeles to the Grand Canyon and all the way to New York City. From the rental car, to hotel bookings, to food and entertainment — everything is prepared. That is, except for one thing: he does not have enough money to go with them.*
>
> *After carefully scripting his plea, he approaches his parents one quiet evening and asks them to sponsor his trip. After all, he asks himself, don't they want me to be happy?*
>
> *Consider the following two scenarios of how the dialogue could unfold.*
>
> **Scenario #1:** *"What did you say — a road trip?! After years of emptying our savings account to send you to college, you want us to pay for your summer vacation across the US?!*

Because you're a mature, young adult, you have our blessing for the trip. But you're going to have to come up with the money on your own...It's time for you to get a job."

Somewhat dejected, Mr. College Graduate applies to the local pizza shop for a full-time, one-month position. He can't miss out on the big trip, so if his parents won't pay for it, he will have to come up with the money on his own.

The first week on the job goes fairly well. Taking the morning, afternoon, and night shifts isn't easy, but his coworkers are friendly and the customers seem happy.

Just three weeks to go, he thinks to himself.

Week Two, however, begins to get a little more challenging. He had to miss a cousin's wedding due to the rigorous work schedule, and his supervisor is upset when he takes a longer-than-scheduled lunch break. Nevertheless, keeping his eye on the big trip ahead makes it all worth it.

Halfway there, he reminds himself, cheering himself on.

While Week Three goes smoothly, Week Four is rather disastrous. He begins to get a little lazy on the job, which gets him into trouble. He mistakenly spills a scalding hot latte on the cash register and lands a fresh, hot pizza splat on the dirty floor. To make matters even worse, he kindly offers a child a free almond cookie, not knowing he has a nut allergy.

His job is switched to dishwasher. Yet, somehow he never gives up; never does he take his eye off the prize — the big unforgettable trip with his friends — a dream which injects him with energy, strength, and even excitement, regardless of how challenging the circumstances.

Finally, he beams with a sense of pride when the store manager hands him his final paycheck. He is ready to hit the road!

Now, let's take a look at a slightly different scenario:

Scenario #2: *"Of course. It would be our pleasure to pay for your road trip. After all, we would do anything to make you happy."*

Question: After which of the two scenarios would we appreciate our trip more? Read the question again. I am not asking which scenario we would initially prefer; rather, I am asking after which scenario would we appreciate our trip more?

Think about it.

At first, our gut feeling may be that we would enjoy both trips equally, but when we think about it again (and apply relevant examples from our lives), we recognize that a trip taken after the first scenario, where we worked for it, would be radically different from one taken after the second scenario.

We would have invested ourselves in it and we would have felt more pride throughout the entire experience. And most importantly, we would have felt as though we earned the trip. It wasn't just a gift or a handout. Rather, it would be something that we deserved because we worked very hard for it.

*And most importantly, we would have felt as though we **earned** the trip. It wasn't just a gift or a handout. Rather, it would be something that we **deserved** because we worked very hard for it.*

It would be the same exact trip with the same exact experiences. But

> without first earning the ability to go, we would have deprived ourselves of a level of pleasure far beyond what it would have been otherwise.
>
> Take a moment. Consider the difference between what we feel when we receive a hard-earned paycheck and when we receive a handout. Even the Talmud reinforces this idea by asserting that a person would prefer one loaf of his own bread over nine loaves from someone else.[6]

Finally, my question was answered, at least at a bird's-eye view. This world is entirely necessary as a vehicle to get to the World to Come. By working to remain a positive, moral, and connected person, notwithstanding our challenges, it is as though we are earning the ultimate eternal paycheck. And by doing so, we are thereby avoiding eternal "unemployment benefits" — which wouldn't be nearly as pleasurable had we not worked for them.

G-d brought each of us to this world, not for His benefit, but entirely for ours. He wants to give us the greatest level of pleasure possible (i.e., the road-trip in the aforementioned analogy) — a level that is only attainable if earned (i.e., the job in the pizza shop).

Hence the need to first be placed in this world and charged with the most sacred task of fulfilling our unique mission. Within this context, we deal with all kinds of adversity. Yet if we keep our eye on the ultimate goal —the ultimate reward — then we have the strength and wherewithal to overcome any challenge sent our way, and even feel meaning and purpose and possibly true happiness during the course of our journey through life.

---

6   *Bava Metzia* 38a.

PRAYER

Another benefit of living in Jerusalem was being right nearby Ari Bensoussan. He was now learning in the Mir Yeshiva, just a ten-minute walk away from Ohr Somayach. He and I took advantage of our close proximity by setting up a biweekly study session in which he would take me through a fascinating exploration of the richness of our daily prayer.

Ari had taken a special interest in prayer, too, perhaps due to his challenges with stuttering and cancer. I felt privileged to learn from him — both as a person and as a teacher.

UNEXPECTED NEWS

Just around that same time, I was shocked to hear news from my doctor. I had been going for X-rays of my spine every few months to ensure that my mild case of scoliosis (curvature of the spine) was in check. Shortly after my transfer to Ohr Somayach, though, the doctor confirmed that I would need to wear a shoulder-to-waist back brace, twenty-three hours a day, for a number of months.

> Wasn't I moving forward in the right direction? Couldn't G-d finally ease up on the hardships and give me a break, allowing me to come closer to Him?

I was flabbergasted. I felt betrayed. I simply couldn't believe it. I was finally coming to terms with my stuttering and other challenges. Wasn't I moving forward in the right direction? Couldn't G-d finally ease up on the hardships and give me a break, allowing me to come closer to Him?

I vividly remember feeling vulnerable and fragile when I was sitting on the hospital gurney, with heavy, warm plaster covering almost my entire body. Again I was crying, but this time out of despair. I was trying so hard to do the right thing, to grow, to be in yeshiva. I was trying so hard to rebuild a once-shattered relationship with G-d. I couldn't comprehend why He was making it so difficult for me to do so. After I had already gone through so much, couldn't He give me some relative comfort so that I could finally focus on learning and growth? Why did it seem like He was pushing me away at a moment when I was truly yearning to come close?

RESILIENCE

I was determined not to give up. Thus, as Ari and I began to study prayer together, I suggested that we start analyzing the section in which we request good health. As I was determined to better understand why G-d would do this to me, I continued to learn, to question, to explore the Torah's response to these timeless queries.

Challenges notwithstanding, I was determined not to flake out. I felt like I had already touched upon what it meant to lead a life with meaning and purpose, and I deeply wanted to better understand the theological challenges that, at face value, seemed to undermine that.

It also gave me comfort to know that I was not the first to experience confusion and frustration in this area of spirituality. Because our greatest scholars throughout history — including Moshe Rabbeinu (Moses) — dealt with this seeming conundrum, I felt validated in my quest to understand what has perhaps been the most perplexing question of all of time: Why do bad things happen to good people?

(Please note: The topic of pain and suffering has a scope far beyond the magnitude of this book. Therefore I merely intend to touch upon a few of the important lessons I learned throughout the years I spent trying find meaning in my stuttering. This is by no means intended to be a comprehensive thesis on the topic. As I explained in the introduction to the book, there are other books I highly recommend that are exclusively focused on this very important subject (see appendix 5.)

Moreover, Jewish thought teaches that while there are a number of theoretical concepts to explain why pain and suffering exist in the world, we never really know for sure why any specific thing happens to a specific person. That is far beyond us. We should rather intellectually reconcile the seeming perplexity around our challenges by recognizing how they could be, and use the renewed understanding as a platform to gain a closer relationship with G-d — through whatever circumstances are sent our way.)

With that in mind, let us now explore two simple fundamental principles which I have learned over the years:

Building Muscle Tone

Consider the following science-fiction analogy:[7]

> An alien lands on planet Earth at the entrance to a building. Curiously, he peeks inside and is dumbfounded. A tough-looking burly man is holding an iron bar over a scrawny, helpless teenager. Just when the teenager seems to be successfully pushing the bar away, the tough-looking, burly man adds more weight onto the bar, seemingly to torture the helpless youth beneath him!

---

7   Based on a *shiur* by Rabbi Benzion Shafier.

The alien frantically looks around for help. He sees many others around, some even watching this take place, but nobody seems to be doing anything to help. He can't fathom the cruelty on planet Earth!

As you may have guessed, the "scrawny, helpless teenager," in reality, hired the "tough-looking, burly man" to be his personal trainer.

Working out is important. Sometimes, it is even enjoyable. Whether it's running, swimming, or lifting weights, we enjoy the exhilaration of it and a deep sense of satisfaction from the end result. Genuine pleasure derived from our exertion cannot be compared to the enjoyment felt by someone who instead decided to stay home, sit on the couch, and watch another movie. While that can be pleasurable, it is on a different level than when we push ourselves to our limit.

This concept can be applied to all of us. G-d is our personal trainer. He knows our true strength and helps us develop it, thereby guiding us along a path to reach our full potential in this world. As a result, the more strenuous the workout, the more laps in the pool and the heavier the weights we can lift, which parallel the greater pleasure we derive from all our efforts.

I had been taught that we are never challenged beyond our capabilities, just like a personal trainer will not push his client beyond his abilities. But to the extent to which we *are* challenged, it is necessary for us to build, grow, and develop our true selves — as deemed necessary by our "Personal Trainer."

GYM VS. SPA

People typically think the world is like a spa, in which we should be able to lead a comfortable, relaxing life. The jacuzzi should be hot, massage therapy available on demand, and cold drinks regularly served. In this world we deserve everything, including health and success. When anything is lacking, therefore, we begin to complain that it's not fair and, Why is this happening to me?

The jacuzzi should be hot, massage therapy available on demand, and cold drinks regularly served. In this world we deserve everything, including health and success.

In reality, however, we are presently in a gym — not a spa — for a relatively short stay, on route to a most luxurious, grandiose, and everlasting spa — otherwise known as the World to Come. In the gym, G-d becomes our personal trainer, helping us tone our muscles and enabling us to grow as strong and fit as we can. He knows our precise body mass and exactly what we are able to handle — nothing more and nothing less. After working out in the gym, we will be allowed entry into the spa to eternally benefit from how we have grown.

This begins to connect back to what we mentioned earlier. The more we work for something, the more we enjoy the reward. In the aforementioned example, he who first engages in a strenuous workout more thoroughly appreciates the privilege of spending time in the spa.

This idea can be further illustrated by comparing it to professional sports. For those in whom he sees the most potential, the coach pushes just a little harder. He knows that by making his star athlete run extra laps and do extra push-ups, he is helping him to become the best player he can be.

From the player's perspective, if he trusts that the coach has his best interests in mind, he is honored to be singled out and is invigorated by the additional challenges. He wants to be a star; he wants to maximize his potential; so he is grateful to the coach for pushing him harder.

As a proud younger brother, I would be remiss if I didn't share the following story:

> My brother, an accountant in Manhattan, balances his days very well: number crunching, running, and family time. He loves it all. One of his greatest accomplishments was when he ran a half-marathon in Miami while pushing a fourteen-year-old wheelchair-bound boy. He knew this boy very well from Chai Lifeline, a nonprofit organization that offers a number of services for Jewish children with life-threatening illnesses, and wanted to help him achieve one of his dreams, that of "running" a half-marathon.
>
> My brother prepared for this race for months in advance. Not only did he have to personally get into shape to run thirteen miles, but he also had to train by pushing an empty wheelchair for miles. What's most interesting, though, is that he didn't feel satisfaction just after the race. Rather, he was invigorated by a sense of mission and purpose throughout the grueling, cold winter mornings that he spent pounding the pavement. He was enthusiastic waking up at four-thirty on the day of the race and he radiated inner joy through every one of the thirteen miles in that race.

Think for a moment: Does that make any sense? He was staying in Miami for the weekend. He could have been relaxing on the beach, sleeping, or doing any other of the myriad (seemingly) more enjoyable activities early that Sunday morning. Why was he so happy running that race?

The point is that when we know that we are working hard for a meaningful cause, we are infused and empowered by it, much more so than by other "easier" activities.

Our deficiency is that we sometimes fail to recognize meaning and purpose behind the challenges we face; we do not always see them as vehicles to reaching our potential in this world. Rather, we tend to see them exclusively as obstacles which prevent us from enjoying and getting what we want out of life.

In fact, it is just the opposite.

When the teenager was working out, he wasn't only bettering his physique and getting exercise. Above and beyond that, he enjoyed — with a deep level of pleasure — every moment of his time with the trainer. Not only that, but did it ever occur to you that people actually pay for personal trainers? We willingly give our hard-earned money to others, asking them to push us to our max.

Great coaches and personal trainers know the limits of their players and clients. G-d is the greatest Coach and Personal Trainer of all. He knows which of our muscles need to be stretched and the body tone that we are capable of achieving. As a result, let us be invigorated by the challenges that we have as we strive to recognize that they are the vehicles through which we can fulfill our potential and ultimately derive the most pleasure possible.

Wisdom Teeth Wisdom

I recently felt discomfort from my upper two wisdom teeth. As suspected, during the ensuing appointment with an oral surgeon, who came highly recommended, he suggested that I have the teeth pulled to prevent the possibility of potential long-term negative effects.

So I did.

The recovery process was incredibly painful and uncomfortable. It took four days for the bleeding to stop and for me to begin eating normally again. But while spending much time in bed holding ice packs to my cheeks, I formulated a deeper understanding of adversity, one that continues to inspire me.

Why would I pay a large sum of money to undergo such a painful procedure? How did I trust a doctor that I had never met before?

The answers are obvious. We know that medical procedures are necessary, even if they cause us discomfort. Although we may not understand exactly what the doctor does, we know that it is ultimately for our benefit. Instead of avoiding the pain now and ignoring the more serious problems that will likely arise in the future, we opt for the short-term pain and prevention.

This concept fascinated me, as it parallels our potential relationship with G-d. If we only viewed G-d as a world-class Doctor, we would be much better off. We would rest assured that whenever we are faced with some form of temporary pain or discomfort, our loving Doctor is performing a procedure on us which will help us in the long run.

PUNISHMENT

The word "punishment" has become unpopular in this day and age. Parents and teachers often find ways to circumvent traditional punishment, and instead focus more on positive reinforcement. That's great. I'm a big fan.

We know, however, that without any sense of discipline, our children would run with abandon, causing great havoc. A "punishment," therefore, can be the greatest gift of all, as it can redirect a child (or student) to the proper path.

G-d does the same with us. He set up a system of reward and punishment to guide His precious creations along a healthy productive path.

Just like the ultimate reward is reserved for the World to Come (as we previously discussed), so too is punishment.

Therefore, in His ultimate kindness, G-d sometimes "punishes" a person in this world for things he's done wrong to save him from the far more severe punishment that is designated for the World to Come. We all make mistakes, and we are accountable for those mistakes. Without properly repenting, justice must be meted out. So when you think about it, wouldn't we prefer some discomfort for a finite period of time (in this world) than a deeper sense of suffering in the World to Come?

Returning to the story above, I realized that the long-term negative effect that my wisdom teeth could have on me far outweighed the short-term discomfort of having them pulled. I had a very real problem and knew it. And so, I chose to have the teeth removed (and I even paid a considerable sum of money to have that done).

Again, if we recognize G-d to be all-loving, only wanting to do what is best for us, shouldn't we then feel appreciative when our metaphorical wisdom teeth are removed, thereby sparing us far more severe, long-term damage?

PARENTAL CRUELTY OR KINDNESS?

The idea of medical procedures leading to increased awareness of G-d's ways brings me to the topic of one of the difficult tasks of parenting: bringing a child to the doctor for shots. I remember my son looking up at me through tears in his eyes, wondering why I was holding him down while a man in a white coat was sharply poking him. After all, didn't I love him? Didn't I care about him? Didn't I want to protect him? How could I be so callous as to allow this total stranger to stick a sharp metal needle into his body?

Nevertheless, as soon as the doctor was done, my son wanted nothing more than to lay his head on my shoulder. While he didn't understand why I had just helped the doctor (seemingly) hurt him, he trusted me; he knew with every fiber of his little being that I was on his side, that I would only do things for his benefit.

A moment like that sheds invaluable insight into our relationship with G-d. After I had my wisdom teeth pulled, I thought: *If I could only thank G-d the way I thanked my oral surgeon.*

After my son cuddled on my shoulder, I thought to myself: *If I could only trust G-d the way my son trusts me.*

With this concept taking shape, we can begin to fathom that maybe, just maybe, every iota of pain and suffering meted out to us in this world is in our best interest. And just like we do not fully understand the exact ingredients in our medications or immunizations, we take them because we know that they are for our good. Therefore, just as I profusely thanked my oral surgeon, should I not also thank G-d for

> *If I could only trust G-d the way my son trusts me.*

the challenges He sends me, even though I don't fully understand how they are for my best?

Perhaps it is for this reason, then, that the Talmud relates that just as we thank G-d for the good in our lives, we thank Him for the "bad" as well.[8] Because if we truly incorporated this all-encompassing framework into our understanding of the inner workings of the world, we would be invigorated by challenges sent our way. Because we would no longer view them as bad; rather, we would begin to see them for what they truly are — the greatest gifts possible.

---

8   *Berachos* 54a.

4

BECOMING HAPPY WITH MYSELF

From the greatest darkness comes the most sublime light.
— *Kabbalah*

LIVING WITH MY back brace was difficult. With metal straps across my stomach, can you imagine the ruckus I constantly caused when walking through metal detectors in Israel? I remember a number of occasions when I was pulled into a side room to actually show them my brace. And due to my broken Hebrew, my attempts to explain its purpose were usually an epic failure.

Moreover, if you are familiar with the Jerusalem summer heat, you can appreciate what it was like to wear a thick, hard plastic brace from my waist up to my shoulders. Because it was brutally uncomfortable, I especially cherished my sports and shower time — the *only* respites I had from the brace.

Slowly but surely, with my newfound approach to life and adversity, I tried to view my brace in a positive light. Occasionally I even tried to laugh, instead of cry, by having some fun with the brace. One particular acquaintance used to introduce me to his friends as the guy with the most impressive stomach muscles. To demonstrate, he encouraged his friends to punch my abdomen as hard as they could.

The result? Priceless.

In a deeper sense, though, I had finally been actualizing the philosophy that I had been learning — in more contexts than just the stuttering.

However, there was still a critical element that was missing: I hadn't fully accepted my challenges. Yes, I was beginning to understand how they could be important and why G-d would give challenges to those He loves. And while that was a huge step from where I had been, I had more room for growth.

I needed to fully accept my stutter, not simply wait impatiently for it to disappear; I needed to accept the fact that I would probably stutter forever, a scary thought that I had been avoiding. Yet if I ever wanted to fully be myself, I needed to regain my optimism, zest for life, and extroverted personality — as a person who stutters.

I wondered if it was even possible…

GROUP THERAPY

My turning point came when I was seventeen years old. I decided to pursue a university degree and felt that it would be best to do so in

America where I could combine an academic degree while still learning in yeshiva. In this transition period, I had two formidable experiences: one was at a unique speech therapy program and the other was as a counselor in Camp HASC.

I heard about the Precision Fluency Shaping Program, a one-month, full-time, intensive speech therapy program that was being offered in Toronto. It was a much sought-after program, one that was designed to completely rewire participants' speech-related motor skills. I assured myself that this would be the last time; this would be the last speech therapy option I would pursue. Afterward, I would just "live life."

The program itself seemed a bit strange, even to me — someone who had already gone through about a decade of speech therapy. Classes were held for about four hours each day and we were given another few hours of homework. Attendance was mandatory, as each step of the program built on the preceding one. Essentially, we were being taught an entirely new method of speech, attempting to uproot our normative speaking habits and replace them with new patterns.

To better understand this, think about someone who, after being involved in an accident, needs physiotherapy to learn how to walk again. The therapist will gradually take him from a sitting position one day to a standing position a few days later, and perhaps after a few weeks, he will begin to guide him to take his first steps, as if he had never walked before.

So, too, the Precision Fluency Shaping Program was designed to rewire participants' motor skills: We spent approximately a week stretching out each vocalized syllable to two

For example, saying "Hi, my name is Moe Mernick" would take more than twenty seconds!

Becoming Happy with Myself 83

seconds apiece, with a one-second breath breaking up each syllable. For example, saying "Hi, my name is Moe Mernick" would take more than twenty seconds! Here is the breakdown:

H-h-i-i-i-i-i-i-i-i (two seconds, plus a one-second breath)
M-m-m-m-y-y-y (two seconds, plus a one-second breath)
n-n-a-a-m-m-e-e (2 seconds, plus a 1-second breath)
i-i-i-i-i-i-s-s-s-s (2 seconds, plus a 1-second breath)
M-m-m-o-o-o-o (2 seconds, plus a 1-second breath)
s-h-e-e-e-e-e-e (2 seconds, plus a 1-second breath)
M-m-m-e-e-e-r-r (2 seconds, plus a 1-second breath)
n-n-n-n-i-i-i-i-c-k (2 seconds, plus a 1-second breath)

As you can imagine, it took a very long time to get any message across. That's what the four hours each day were for!

We were all able to instantly relate to one another, laugh at ourselves, and realize the similarity in our stuttering patterns, as well our various coping methods.

But we had fun. It was my first time in a group speech therapy setting, with about eight participants in total. We were all able to instantly relate to one another, laugh at ourselves, and realize the similarity in our stuttering patterns, as well our various coping methods. It was fascinating and comforting for me to realize that I was not alone, that there were others like me — working in business, the arts, and other professions — who were able to lead fulfilling lives beyond their teenage years, notwithstanding the severity of their stutter.

Why had I not been exposed to others like these people before? It would have been very helpful. To laugh together, to cry together — it made me feel better that I was not alone. Parenthetically, this is actually one of the reasons I am now sharing my story: I do not want anyone to experience that loneliness or to feel that nobody can relate to their stutter.

"SLOW NORMAL"

In the Precision Fluency Shaping Program, we gradually moved to speaking in one-second syllables, followed by half-second ones and then finally in "slow normal" speed, incorporating the patterns we had learned along the way.[9]

Toward the end of the program, I felt frustrated that I was not able to speak with the level of fluency I was hoping for, or rather, expecting. Therefore, after class one day, I expressed my dissatisfaction to Lori, the program facilitator, complaining about my stuttering and how it might never go away (as I really hoped it would). At that moment, I was on the verge of giving up; it just seemed too overwhelming to project ahead on a life of stuttering when I had built up my expectation that this program would help me become completely fluent.

Her response — simple yet profound, warm yet insistent — has stuck with me since:

> Moe, you have so much going for you. You're smart, good-looking, athletic, and easy to get along with. Yes, you also have a stutter. It is part of the package. You must accept your package in order to move on with your life. Wallowing in the fact that you have a speech impediment will not help anything or anyone. Only once you embrace whatever you have been given — yes, that means every aspect of that package — can you truly lead a happy life.

---

[9] While this method has helped a number of people, some feel that it is an unnatural and unsustainable way to speak, thereby dropping many of the key takeaways from the intensive program.

Wow, I thought. *She was right.* And as much as I may have heard similar thoughts from others in various forms, it never hit home the way it did during that conversation. Perhaps it was the timing, perhaps it was the frustration, or maybe it was because I was at the point of almost giving up and I was thus vulnerable and open to a powerful answer.

Whatever the case may be, Lori's emphatic message gave me a much-needed boost. Even though I had come to intellectually accept G-d as the all-knowing and loving Benefactor behind my stutter, I had yet to cross the chasm to feeling totally comfortable with my speech habits. Lori's message, however, was the impetus for this change. No longer was stuttering going to be something that I avoided at all costs; no longer would stuttering be something I hid away in a dark place, only allowing it to surface inside my comfort zones with the people I felt at ease with. I was seventeen years old. It was time for me to get out there; it was time for me to live a little bit more; it was time for me to break out of my shell, to stop stifling my true personality and allow my true colors to finally shine.

THE STONE CUTTER

This universal message reminded me of the classic story of the stone cutter.[10]

> *There was once a stone cutter who spent his time, day in and day out, monotonously chiseling stone from a quiet, deserted mountaintop. How he longed for a different life — a life where he would feel more important, a life where people would recognize his existence.*

---

10   I originally heard this story from R' David Shaw, while we were teaching together on an educational program for high school students in Australia.

One day, the king's royal entourage was passing on the road below and caught his attention. Surrounded by dozens of courtiers and hundreds of enthusiastic onlookers, the king seemed to have everything — honor, glory, and wealth. The stone cutter, coveting the king's lot in life, gazed intently from the mountain above. How he wished to wield that ultimate power; how he wished to experience that kind of luxury; how he wished to be the king.

POOF!

The following morning, when the stone cutter awoke, he was shocked to find himself in the palace! His jewel-studded throne awaited his presence, while his servants began serving him delicacies he had never before seen. *This is the life*, he told himself. *I am the most powerful man in the world!*

For the next few weeks, he spared no expense living his dreams and exercising his power by conquering neighboring countries. He truly lived like a king.

However, after some time, he began to feel extremely uncomfortable. The palace seemed to be baking in the intense heat of the summer sun that penetrated the palace walls, and this made the king very hot. The king began to suffer in his heavy velvet royal robes and he could find no enjoyment.

If only I was the sun, he wished. *Then, as the most powerful force in the world, I would finally be happy.*

POOF!

The next day, the stone cutter-turned-king found himself to be the sun. By shining down with all of his might on those he disliked and providing pleasant sunshine to his loved ones, he thoroughly enjoyed his unparalleled power. Nobody is more powerful than me, he reassured himself. I am finally happy.

This lasted but a few days until the clouds came along and blocked his ability to shine on certain parts of the world. Nothing he did could displace those clouds. Ugh! he said to himself. Just when I thought I was the most powerful force in the world. I wish I was a cloud!

And, yes, POOF!

Blowing indiscriminately at humans below, the stone cutter-turned-king-turned-sun-turned-cloud finally felt like he had reached the ultimate in this world. While dancing through the sky all day long, he could either greatly enhance people's lives by providing them with a nice, cool breeze or he could decide to ruin people's lives by blowing harder and causing indiscriminate destruction. Who could be more powerful than me? he wondered, with an arrogant chuckle.

The mountain, however, proved him wrong. It just wouldn't budge. No matter what the wind did, the mountain remained unchanged, unaffected by the wind's might. In despair, the stone cutter cried out, "If only I could be the mountain, then I'm sure I would be happy!"

POOF.

And happy he was, totally on top of the world.

Until, one day, he felt a light chipping on his back. The incessant noise and splintering irritated him immensely, but there was nothing he could do about it. Taking a peek over his shoulder, there stood a stone cutter, happily doing his job...

THOU SHALT NOT...

As humans, we have an innate tendency to look at others and covet their lot in life. Whether it is our neighbors, colleagues, or distant cousins, others seem to have it so much better than we do. And often, we secretly desire to lead their lives, instead of charting our own.

We cannot be entirely blamed for this. There is a multibillion dollar advertising industry that is entirely focused on making us feel like we would "finally be happy if" we could have the latest smartphone, go on that luxurious vacation, or lose those additional ten pounds. From jewelry to cuisine, we are bombarded with strategically placed messages that brainwash us into thinking that our lives are not complete without the advertised product or service. Society at large feeds into our vulnerability as well, manipulating us to feel that self-esteem is a direct result of our physical appearance and social status.

With this in mind, I was deeply troubled by a question. Judaism's tenth of the Ten Commandments reads: "You shall not covet." I shall not...what? How can I be commanded to control an emotion, a subconscious instinct? Jealousy is a part of the natural fabric of human beings. Ultimately, we all want the best life possible. We want to be as happy as we can be. And as such, our emotions pull us after others who seem to have life happening in their favor. How can I be expected to control a spontaneous feeling?

> *I shall not...what? How can I be commanded to control an emotion, a subconscious instinct?*

Ibn Izra, a brilliant twelfth-century commentator, teaches us an invaluable lesson: What is allocated to us should be used to fulfill our mission on Earth; everything else is withheld from us because it will only distract us from our true purpose.[11] Thus, we should perceive everything outside our lot as beyond our realm. In addition to assigning us a unique mission and purpose, G-d equipped us with the necessary tools to fulfill our role in this world. Therefore, each variable in our lives was purposefully placed to enable us to maximize our time in this world. Coveting another person's car, job, or spouse is undermining this fundamental principle. At the same time, appreciating all the different facets of our lives enables us to not only gain a deeper relationship with the Creator of the world, but also helps us channel our unique strengths and talents into becoming the best people we can be, all the while avoiding negative, unproductive jealousy.

So just like the stone cutter in the previous story, if we focus on using our various talents and skills to fulfill our mission, not only will we be well on our way to doing so, but we will also be spared from jealousy, the virus which poisons mankind and, as Rabbi Elazar HaKappar comments, removes us from truly "living" in this world.[12]

FREEDOM FROM ENVY

In his book *My Father, My King*, Rabbi Zelig Pliskin suggests the following imagery:[13]

> Hear your Father, your King, the Creator and Sustainer of the entire universe, saying to you:
> "I have given you, and will continue to give you, exactly what you need to fulfill your mission in this world. This awareness

---

11   *Shemot* 20:14.
12   *Pirkei Avot* 4:28.
13   Rabbi Zelig Pliskin, *My Father, My King* (Brooklyn: Mesorah Publications, 1999), 73–75.

will free you from envy. You have your unique set of tools; no one else's tools are needed for your life's mission.

"I want you to live a joyous life. This is only possible if you experience joy with what I have given you. Envy destroys a person's life. It prevents you from enjoying what you have.

"Focus on people who have less than you and still live a joyous life. This will teach you that you, too, can live a joyous life in spite of not having everything you want.

"Even in the realm of service to Me, keep your main focus on what you personally can do to serve Me to the best of your ability. Don't allow anyone else's accomplishments to cause you distress. Just the opposite. If someone does something special, learn from him. At the same time, realize that I have made each of My children special and unique. Each child has unique talents, skills, and life circumstances. Don't compare yourself with others. Serve me with your own intelligence, your own emotions, and your own unique circumstances.

"Much of the envy in the world is based on mistaken perceptions. You can't judge the true extent of a person's fortune by outward appearances. Some of the people whom you might envy are simultaneously envying you. And if you knew their situations in their entirety, you would realize that you have nothing to be jealous of.

"I want you to experience so much joy and pleasure with what I have given you that there will be no room left to feel bad because of what someone else has. I have given you a multitude of good things from which to derive enjoyment and benefit. You will always have many things for which to feel thankful. Take *pleasure in what you have. When you use your mind properly, you will see what a wonderful life is yours to live."*

Love,

Your Father in Heaven

A HAPPIER ME?

If I wanted to lead a happier life, it was necessary to incorporate the messages from Lori, the stone cutter, and the Torah itself. Still, formulating my thinking around these principles was not easy. It went against twelve years of negative speaking and thinking patterns. It was no simple task to begin socializing freely or reading from the Torah, nor was it natural to stop being jealous of other people's fluency.

Intellectually, I knew that I should accept my stutter; practically, however, it was very difficult. As much as I tried to incorporate them into my day-to-day life, I could not fully bring myself to accept all of the long-term implications. Indeed, I knew that if I could only live by Lori's wise words, I would be more at peace with myself, I would be able to let go of a lot of my anger, and ultimately, I would be a much happier person.

How to do this, however, still baffled me. How to enthusiastically look forward to a life filled with constant struggle and embarrassment eluded me. I knew that I would always be me. But sadly, I still wasn't that thrilled with who that was. Couldn't I simply choose to keep certain parts of me, while conveniently leaving out others?

It took at least two years for these ideas to take root. And even once they did, it was still by no means an easy or comfortable process. But positive change must be steady and organic, and that is the path I decided to take.

CAMP HASC

Following my full-time enrollment in the Precision Fluency Shaping Program (and before going to yeshiva in Waterbury), I worked as a counselor at Camp HASC, a summer program for individuals with special needs. Notwithstanding my lack of experience in this area, the camp entrusted me, along with my five co-counselors, to care for six young (mostly autistic) campers who were unable to verbally communicate.

Twenty-four hours a day, my co-counselors and I served as our campers' friends, counselors, and parents. Functioning on very little sleep, we were challenged to constantly prioritize the needs and comforts of our campers before our own. Showering, feeding, and changing campers' diapers were activities that became second nature to us. This was very new to me.

At four o'clock in the morning, for instance, if one of our campers needed to be showered and his bed changed, we were the only ones who could fulfill those duties. In addition, because most of our campers were unable to speak, we quickly learned effective non-verbal communication skills which worked far better than we ever could have imagined.

Camp HASC is known as a "magical oasis" for individuals with special needs. However, only after putting my heart and soul into my campers did I realize that it was magical not only for the campers, but for the counselors as well. Many campers return home from their HASC experience having taken their very first steps or spoken their very first words. Many counselors return home from their HASC experience having selflessly devoted themselves to the needs of others and having evolved into much more sensitive, giving, and grateful people as a result.

In my case, this could not have been more true. From my summer at HASC (and subsequent year-round involvement with the special-needs community), I learned that the most difficult undertakings in life are oftentimes the most rewarding. After my first week at HASC, I seriously considered leaving early. Never before had I felt such physical and emotional exhaustion.

> *I learned that the most difficult undertakings in life are oftentimes the most rewarding.*

Despite that, or perhaps *because* of that, I pushed even harder. Moe was not going to be a quitter. It was only then that the extreme demands of my charges revealed levels of sensitivity and depth of caring I never knew I possessed.

Moreover, I experienced what could be described as an absolute, genuine satisfaction from working with my campers, despite the lack of conventional thank-yous from them, since they were simply unable to verbally express their appreciation. Just how does one measure, for instance, a goodbye hug from an autistic camper who rarely expressed his emotions? How does one begin to quantify that all-encompassing message of gratitude and love?

> *Just how does one measure, for instance, a goodbye hug from an autistic camper who rarely expressed his emotions?*

Quitting after my first three days at HASC would have been much easier, but would have left me a much poorer person. Because once I acclimated, my HASC experience was one of heightened patience, sensitivity, selflessness, and the resolve to succeed, all unquestionably vital to my personal and professional development.

WHY VS. HOW

My turnaround at HASC resulted from a paradigm shift. Instead of dwelling on the adversity that my campers and their families faced all year round, I began to focus on my task at hand: recognizing that my campers' parents needed a respite (for themselves, as well as in order to spend quality time with each other and/or their other children) and to provide my campers with the summer of a lifetime.

Once I was able to internalize that message, I was able to finally flourish as a counselor. It was no longer about *why*, it was rather about *how*. How can I help make this an awesome summer for my campers?

This was an important message, one that resonated with me throughout the summer. Applying it to my life, too, was a big step. Perhaps it was time to stop harping on the *why* and to begin focusing instead on the *how*. No longer should I be frustrated, even angry, about why I stutter, but rather I should channel that energy into contemplating how I could lead a happy, productive, and meaningful life as someone who stutters.

My summer at Camp HASC helped me take a step back and realize how much time and energy I spent worried and upset by my stutter, for naught. My campers, who had far more serious lifelong challenges than I did, had a sparkle in their eyes and a true zest for life. They appreciated the small things, much of which I was taking for granted.

Another paradigm shift, if I may, came for me during the quieter evening hours, which were conducive to introspection. I thought about my stutter and how it had held me back for so many years. Then I realized that yes, I had a stutter...but most of my campers could not speak at all. And somehow, this did not impede their ability to appreciate life. Why couldn't I do the same?

The summer at HASC, therefore, was a pivotal period in my life, one that was strategically placed — "coincidentally," right after my memorable talk with Lori during the Precision Fluency Shaping Program.

Not only did I begin forcing myself into social situations to break out of my shell, but, more importantly, I also began to look beyond myself at the larger picture. I began to see that life can be more meaningful and intrinsically beautiful through the challenges that we face. Moreover, I learned that the greatest pleasure is earned through hard work; following my seven exhausting weeks at HASC, I felt better about myself than I ever had before.

As they say, life is short and there is much to accomplish. There was no time for me to live in isolation and pity myself. Instead, I was determined to find ways to continue to grow, both in my outlook and the way I took action. I was determined to live the fully enriched, uncut version of my life, one unimpeded by the fear of my stutter.

The more I was able to appreciate all the different aspects that comprised who I was (my adversity included), the less I felt compelled to covet what others had. Unlike the stone cutter in the aforementioned story, I stopped thinking about how much happier I would be if only I had those qualities. More and more, I was appreciating my unique lot in life, beginning to recognize that greatness is attainable through my challenges, not despite them.

Speaking of appreciating one's lot in life, it is crucial to emphasize this point a bit more.[14] Imagine the following scenario:

> An acclaimed actor receives a call from his agent.
> "I have great news! I just received the perfect script for you; it's a guaranteed Oscar. I want you to look it over immediately."

---

14   Based on a *shiur* by Rabbi Benzion Shafier.

After carefully reviewing the script, the actor calls his agent back. "Bob, I looked it over. Forget it; I'm not taking the role."

"What's going on?! Why don't you want it?" replies the bewildered agent.

"I'm not doing it. Period."

"Is it the script?"

"No, the script is fine."

"Is it the other actors?"

"Nope. They're fine."

"Do you need more money? I'm sure we can get that for you!"

"Nope, the pay is fine."

"So what can it be?"

"Don't you get it? The guy they'd have me playing is a loser, a fool — down and out."

"But it's just the part. It's not you..."

"But by doing this part, millions of people will see me as such an unpopular guy. I can't stand the embarrassment. I'm not doing it. Period!"

HOW ARE WE JUDGED?

Now obviously, this conversation never took place. Any actor or moviegoer understands that it is not the actual person being defined by the role; it is all staged. As such, it is universal knowledge that the actor's success is judged by one criteria, and one criteria alone: how well he plays his part.

If his part is to play the role of a fool, and he plays it well, he will win awards and go on to fame. If his part is to play the role of the most successful, wealthy person on the planet, but he does not play it well, the critics will shred him to pieces.

He is not judged by how much money the actor in the role has; he is not judged by how tall or handsome the script says he should be. Again, he is judged by one single criteria: how well he played his part.

This may sound simple, but it is also a fundamental principle in life. We are placed in this world with a role to fulfill, a mission to accomplish. And at the end of our lives, we will be judged by only one criteria: how well we played our role.

Sadly, we often get so caught up in the nuances of the role itself, with the "props" around us, losing sight of the true goal of maximizing our potential.

Paralleling the analogy, I began to internalize this idea. Like everyone around me, I did not choose most of my life circumstances. I did not choose the generation into which I was born, the family dynamic into which I was placed, or my IQ level. Many of my "stage settings" — including my stutter — were things I was born into. These were decided for me, without my input. What I *am* given full control over, however, is how I can ultimately maximize the life into which I was placed.

Much of what people take credit for in life has little to do with them. Not only is one's family's status predetermined, but his inborn temperament and disposition are not variables that are chosen either; they are given to each person at birth.

But here is the punch line. These very qualities were given to us to help us fulfill our mission. As a hand fits a glove, we were placed into our lives, but not arbitrarily nor by happenstance. Before we were put into this world, G-d intricately designed the circumstances of our entire lives. And so, we are placed into the perfect setting for us to achieve our unique kind of perfection in this world.

Each "setting" has a unique set of challenges — wealth on the one hand and poverty on the other; intelligence on the one hand and a lack thereof on the other; fluent speech on the one hand and stuttering on the other. None is fundamentally better or worse; they are all different dynamics that help guide us to fulfill our unique mission of self-perfection.

Simplemindedly, we look at successful people as though G-d loves them and unsuccessful people as though He does not. We cannot be more mistaken. Analyzing the lives of any of our historic leaders proves this notion wrong; the greatest Jews in history had perhaps the most difficult challenges.

While at Camp HASC, I began asking *how* and not *why*. Then, as I began to internalize these new concepts, I focused on how I could best play my part in this world — using all the stage settings that I had been given to do so.

5

TAKING ACTION

Don't tell G-d how big your problems are;
tell your problems how big G-d is!

— Unknown

A CLEAR MANIFESTATION OF my growth was epitomized by my breakthrough in prayer. For years, I had great difficulty with prayer. Hundreds, if not thousands, of heartfelt prayers were dedicated toward my stutter, praying for it to disappear, begging G-d to mercifully remove this impediment which I often felt was taking over my life and not allowing me to be the "normal" teenager that I so desperately wanted to be. Day after day, week after week, month after month, and year after year, it was becoming quite frustrating that my stuttering constantly hindered my ability to be my true self.

Weren't my heartfelt prayers being heard? If there was truly Someone up there listening to me, why wasn't He answering? Were more tears necessary? How many more jokes would have to be made about me before He would take notice? Finally, I had occasionally wondered, *Was He even listening?!*

Over time, my heartfelt supplications had shifted toward expressions of anger — or, even worse, no expression at all; total disinterest.

But shortly after Camp HASC, my approach changed. I had just enrolled in the Yeshiva Gedolah of Waterbury, nestled in the beautiful rolling hills of Connecticut, where I would combine my Torah learning with an undergraduate college degree. The learning had certainly kicked up a notch from my time at Ohr Somayach and my new rabbis were outstanding, both in terms of their warmth and their knowledge, and I began to create long-lasting meaningful friendships with some incredible, like-minded people.

As this was unfolding, I had a discussion with my rabbi in which I expressed to him my new revolutionary (for me, at least) approach to prayer. I told him:

> *The nature of my prayers has recently changed. No longer do I simply beg G-d to take away my stuttering. Rather, I begin my personal requests similar to how they began in the past, expressing how painful it is to stutter and how helpful it would be if it vanished, disappeared without a trace, never to be heard of again. I explain how appreciative I would be if He would do so. After all, if He can create an entire universe, surely He can get rid of my stutter.*

But my prayers didn't stop there. Instead of ending every prayer service with the inflated hope of being able to speak fluently, I included the following important addendum:

> G-d, You created not only the world around me, but You created me, too. You know me better than I could ever imagine; You know who came before me, who will come after me, and all the ramifications of my life, from beginning to end. Therefore, I trust You. I trust that You are taking care of me, just like You have taken care of me for the last eighteen years. You have given me so many blessings in my life, and I am so grateful. And because You know me so well, You know how much the stuttering pains me; You know how much I have dreamed about being able to speak "regularly." You know. You've been listening.
>
> Therefore, knowing what You know, if You still see true purpose in my stutter and will therefore leave it as is, then I ask You but one favor: Please equip me with the strength to handle it. Again, if You have to answer no to my previous requests based on reasons that I am unable to comprehend, then I respectfully demand the strength and positivity that are necessary for me to make the best of it.
>
> I want to live life to its fullest. I want to be able to speak without feeling inhibited by my speech impediment. No longer do I want to shy away from social situations out of fear of embarrassment. I ask that You help me leave all that behind me.
>
> If stuttering is what's best, then please help me recognize it as such by providing me with the strength, wisdom, and resources to grow from it.

That was transformational. No longer was my stuttering "a mistake"; no longer was it an "impediment" in the truest sense of the word, for it no longer impeded my ability to reach the highest heights possible. After all, if G-d intended for me to stutter, greatness must be possible within the context of my stutter. No longer did I hope to achieve greatness in my life *despite* my stutter; rather, I hoped to achieve greatness in my life *as a result of* my stutter. No longer was I arrogantly telling G-d how I need to be designed; rather, I was recognizing that He is running the world in the best way possible, with my best interests in mind. And if that included a stutter, then I was praying for the humility to accept it.

Clearly, I had a part to play in this world, and if that part included a stutter, then it became my goal to play that part as best as I could — because that is the sole criteria on which I will be judged.

ART BERG

Art Berg's inspirational story wonderfully illustrates this concept. At the age of twenty-one, Art's "normal" life came screeching to a halt, as he found himself in a car accident that almost completely paralyzed him. As a quadriplegic, he had only a little control over his arms — nothing more.

His popular book — *The Impossible Just Takes a Little Longer: Living with Purpose and Passion* (William Morrow Paperbacks, 2003) — describes his incredible story. Despite the odds, Art went on to become a well-known speaker, formed two companies, wrote three books, and became an international success story.

One of the most fascinating parts of his life is that shortly after the doctors told him that he would never walk again, he made a seemingly ludicrous comment, "I will win a Superbowl ring."

And yes, two short years before he passed away, he was, in fact, awarded with a Superbowl ring. The Baltimore Ravens' coach claims that the thirty-fifth Superbowl victory was attributable to Art Berg. The Ravens had been performing poorly and they invited Art to give them a pep talk at the beginning of the season. Apparently, his motivational talk charged the players and his inspirational words became their mantra. As a result, they attributed their subsequent victory to him by awarding him with his dream come true — a Superbowl ring.

What is even more interesting, though, is that some years into his successful career, he began to reflect back on the four months he spent in the hospital following his accident. He was puzzled as to why he always had a private room, why therapists always seemed to frequent his bedside, and why the nurses tried to keep family away.

Exploring the documentation from the hospital, he found his answer: He had been diagnosed with a unique psychological condition — excessive happiness. He would joke and laugh and seemed to be in a perpetually good mood. The psychiatrist assigned to his case assumed, therefore, that he was partly delusional, that he did not fully understand his new depressing reality. After all, how could a previously healthy twenty-one year old — recently turned quadriplegic — remain in good spirits?

What happened?

Art explains that he had made a conscious decision to be happy. He resolved to lead a passionate, meaningful life, and would not allow his new condition to inhibit him from doing so. Thus, in a wheelchair, with limited use of his arms, he became not just enthusiastic about the opportunities ahead of him, but also productive and impactful.

If you could go back in time, would you do it all over again?

At the end of his book, he shares a poignant question that his friends often asked him: Art, if you could go back in time, would you have flown on an airplane instead of driving your car? If you could go back in time, would you do it all over again?

Art responded honestly; he said he wasn't sure. But his answer came at a later date, while he was on an airplane that hit a dangerous patch of turbulence. With his life flashing before his eyes, Art realized that if he could go back and actively choose his circumstances all over again, he would. His accident had made him become a much happier person. He was quoted as saying, "It was the greatest thing that ever happened to me."

IF ONLY

When we wallow in our misery, we have only ourselves to blame. Our circumstances too often dictate our mood. How many of us have made any of the following flippant statements:

> *If only I had more money...*
> *If only I was smarter...*
> *If only I was healthier...*
> *If only I had more friends...*
> *If only I didn't stutter...*
> *...then I'd be happy!*

The words "if only" should be removed from our lexicon. Not only are we unable to change certain variables in our lives, but by fantasizing about circumstances that are not ours, we fail to recognize that those challenges placed in our path are often what can bring us the most meaning, purpose, and happiness in life.

> *The words "if only" should be removed from our lexicon.*

Like Art, I realized that I should capitalize on my challenges; I should leverage them to become a better person. Because they were given to me for a reason, I should stop focusing on trying to get rid of them and instead focus on how to take advantage of them, how to focus on the opportunity in them. I decided to try to be more like Art Berg and to begin to view life from his vantage point.

PUBLIC SPEAKING

It was time for me to take action. Even as I began to intellectually understand that the challenge of stuttering was designed for me, to help me reach my potential in this world, actualizing that reality, amidst continued pain and embarrassment, was still not easy. Necessary, yet difficult.

During my time at university, there was simply no way to circumvent the prerequisite public speaking course. (Someone once advised me to skip university altogether because I would have to take that course. Terrible advice!) There was no way of getting around the fact that I was required to deliver a speech every second class, just like all the other students. Gripped with horror, I approached the professor and explained my plight. Respectfully, he responded that while there is no way of circumventing the actual speeches, he would take my stuttering into account with regard to my grades.

There is a well-known adage: The second biggest fear among people is dying; the first, though, is public speaking. Therefore, when on the first day of class the professor required each of us to introduce ourselves from the podium, I remember feeling how much, at that moment, I would have preferred to be six feet under.

Despite the modest classroom size, this still meant public speaking — better known as SPEAKING IN PUBLIC! This was something I hadn't been forced to do in years, and was *not* something I wanted to try. Indeed, I wanted to overcome my fear of speaking, but not at the risk of embarrassing myself in front of all my classmates. I just wanted the stuttering to go away, not to actually undergo a painful process to help get rid of it.

While it took the other students about twenty seconds each to provide a brief personal overview, it took me almost ten times as long. The words just would not come out. (Whether you stutter or have seen others do so, you are probably familiar with all types of face contortions and tongue jerking that accompany a vicious stutter. To put it lightly, it was not fun.)

> *While it took the other students about twenty seconds each to provide a brief personal overview, it took me almost ten times as long. The words just would not come out.*

But to make matters even worse, I wasn't just stuttering in front of one or two people, as I was accustomed to doing. I was at a podium in a classroom; all eyes were on me. I was mortified.

After what seemed like an eternity, I took my seat and watched the next student whiz his way through his introduction. Instead of feeling sorry for myself, though, I tried very hard to remind myself of my seemingly incomprehensible accomplishment: I had just spoken in front of a crowd!

My subsequent speeches, as well, took longer than the other students. Interestingly, though, as the semester rolled along, I gradually developed a comfort zone in the classroom and began speaking with more confidence and less of a stutter. The speeches even became more enjoyable. To this day, I have pleasant memories of this course and I vividly recall presentations I delivered.

Ever since my one-off bar mitzvah speech, public speaking was taboo in my world. As such, there was a unique energy that I felt while standing in front of my classmates. Even though I was still speaking with a stutter, the comfort zone I developed in the classroom began making my speeches enjoyable. It felt like I was finally emerging out of the safe, insulated cocoon I had created for myself.

I was beginning to love it.

> *It felt like I was finally emerging out of the safe, insulated cocoon I had created for myself.*

COMFORT ZONE

Perhaps the most unique element of stuttering, contrasted with other speech impediments, is its inconsistency. For comparison's sake, if one has a lisp, he will always lisp on certain sounds, including when he is singing or talking to himself.

Not so with stuttering.

It is fascinating to note that a person will never stutter when he sings or speaks to himself, but usually stutters in speaking situations when anxiety levels are high. Researchers scramble in various directions to detail the complexities of one's brain in their efforts to explain why stuttering is nonexistent in these situations. Yet no clear answer is given. Fascinating, isn't it?

Thus, the safe zone that I developed in my Public Speaking classroom was very healthy. From the first day when I introduced myself at the podium, everyone knew that I had a severe stutter. After that, there were no other surprises throughout the semester we spent together.

Similarly, if one has a close relationship with a parent, sibling, or friend, the stutter will rarely manifest itself in conversations with that person.

Comfort zones can be built and developed, as became the case in my public speaking classroom. Because everyone came to know (very well) that I had a stutter, the anxiety level built around stuttering greatly diminished. No longer did I have the all too familiar thoughts: What if I stutter? What will they think of me? What can I do to avoid the stutter? Oh no, I am going to stutter!

> No longer did I have the all too familiar thoughts: What if I stutter? What will they think of me? What can I do to avoid the stutter? Oh no, I am going to stutter!

There was nothing to hide. I could be myself. Whether I stuttered or not made no difference. This was the first time in my life I felt comfortable speaking aloud in a group setting. And interestingly, as a result, the frequency and severity of my stutter patterned my decreasing anxiety; the less nervous I was to actually stutter, the less I did. As a result, the class became a safe haven for me to begin honing my rusty, if-ever-existent public speaking skills.

It was liberating; it felt awesome!

JOB SEEKING

It was now time to put my newly developed confidence and public speaking skills to the test.

During my last year at university, I interviewed for an internship at a large, reputable financial firm. The interview was nerve-racking, as you can imagine. But somehow, because I managed to steer the discussion in a way which had the interviewer talking mostly about himself and his hobbies, I escaped unscathed — without speaking much, and therefore with little to no stuttering — and with an offer!

It was super exciting. At the same time, however, I was nervous, as my supervisor wasn't aware of my stutter. And because I was still embarrassed by its implications, I wasn't exactly prepared to enlighten him with that information. (Reflecting back, it is clear that my confidence level at that stage had improved from earlier years, but was still not ideal. I should definitely have been more open about my stutter during my interview.)

My supervisor initially built up my role to sound like I would actually be performing important functions, such as financial and portfolio analysis, but in actuality, I wound up doing what many college interns do, i.e., photocopying papers and fetching coffee. Yet, within that framework there was still some client interaction, whether that meant handling certain calls or welcoming clients to the office.

My desk was set up in the corner of my supervisor's large, corner office and I vividly remember my utter fear when I was expected to make calls in his presence. All the usual stuttering anxiety was at its best. After all, how could I stutter at this prim, proper, and otherwise perfect financial firm? What if I came across as unprofessional to a client? Would my supervisor still be willing to write me a glowing recommendation for my graduate school application?

Nearly a decade later, I still recall the tension. It felt as though I was constantly walking on eggshells, trying to circumvent any situation in which my stuttering could pose a problem.

Nearly a decade later, I still recall the tension. It felt as though I was constantly walking on eggshells, trying to circumvent any situation in which my stuttering could pose a problem. This avoidance, though, was very unproductive and became a vicious cycle. The more I avoided situations in which I thought I might stutter, the more I stuttered when I was put into those situations.[15]

Disappointed, I thought to myself, *Hadn't I been practicing giving speeches at university? How did my newly developed self-confidence erode? If I had become more comfortable with my stutter (as I began to understand that G-d was sending it for my growth and development), why couldn't I carry myself more confidently? Why did I feel the need to hide it so much? Most importantly, why wasn't I feeling happier with myself?*

I had come so far. But, clearly, there was still a distance to go.

CENTRAL EUROPE

Overall, the internship went smoothly and was a positive experience. My boss liked me and his partner expressed interest in having me continue with the firm following my graduation from university. However, something didn't feel right. My natural disposition had been replaced with a more timid and quiet one. I didn't like it at all. I knew I needed something else.

As such, when the opportunity arose to volunteer in Germany for seven weeks, I enthusiastically grabbed it.

Organized through the Yeshiva Gedolah of Waterbury, three friends and I were selected to participate in The Bridge of Understanding, a German non-profit program geared toward introducing North American Jewish college students to the modern-day complexities of the relationship between Germany and Israel in the twenty-first century. Based in Berlin, we were to spend approximately two months

---

15 Refer to chapter 1, where I discussed how difficult it was for me to say my name, telephone number, and "hello" — all words that were now unavoidable in a high-pressured environment.

not only traveling the country to meet with politicians and discuss critical issues, but also to leverage our Jewish education to teach local Jewish youth who attended different programs sponsored by the Ronald S. Lauder Foundation.

Right away, I was thrown into unfamiliar territory, such as delivering lectures to high school and college students. Yet surprisingly, I thrived. It was almost as if I took on a whole new persona. But it wasn't just because I was in a different part of the world where nobody knew of my stuttering past. Rather, I extended myself beyond my normal comfort zone and I was resolute not to avoid new opportunities, regardless of any impediment I felt I had.

My new resolution was: I was going to be me. No shying away from situations, no feeling sorry for myself, and no second-guessing G-d about His master plan. I was in a new continent, where nobody had any preconceived notions about me or my speech habits. I was determined to come across comfortable with who I was, stutter included.

Perhaps I was also gaining confidence from the fact that my nationality was a novelty and my attempts to speak German were highly appreciated (in an entertaining way). Whatever it was, I was loving it.

While the initial signs of my speech becoming more fluent may have been visible during my public speaking course at university, they began to sprout in Germany. Everything seemed like it was coming together. While based in Berlin, I traveled extensively to Hamburg, Leipzig, and Munich for different educational programs, and I was often encouraged to deliver impromptu speeches to all kinds of audiences.

> *I still stuttered, but it didn't matter as much.*

I still stuttered, but it didn't matter as much. I remember it feeling surreal. It was as though I was being reborn, invigorated to give life another shot — this time, though, as myself. No more hiding. No more pretending to be someone I was not. My dream of confidently living my life was finally coming true.

FULL DISCLOSURE

As I developed my self-confidence at the podium, it gave me the strength and wherewithal to be up front about my stutter — a tactic which has been enormously effective to this very day.

I like to call it "full disclosure" and it usually goes something like this: "Before I begin, I just want to let you know that I have a stutter, which means that I may get caught on certain words. It's pretty outgoing, so it may pop up to introduce itself."

There we go. It's out there. Those of us who stutter know that during a conversation, a certain degree of comfort is felt when the other party knows about our stutter. In those situations, our anxiety is usually less debilitating. We can focus on the actual words we would like to use to express ourselves, rather than obsessing exclusively on avoiding the words that we fear will trip us up.

Before that critical milestone, though, anxiety would take on a life of its own: *What will they think of me? How will they respond? What can I do to avoid stuttering? Maybe I'll just keep quiet instead.* After spending my whole life feeling closeted by my fear of speaking, my new full-disclosure practice in Germany helped me feel like I had finally burst through the stage doors, ready to perform. Jumping at additional opportunities to speak and teach, I found myself again and again honing my skills at the beginning of a presentation, lecture, or class with a slight comment or joke about my stuttering, before zeroing in on the topic at hand.

Was it that simple? I wondered.

It struck me that nearly two years after my conversation with Lori, I was finally actualizing her wake-up call. I was comfortable enough with my stutter not to allow it to impede my life, and I was embracing my stutter by being confident enough to joke about it with others, indicating a healthy acceptance of the challenge I'd lived with all that time. I was finally at ease with my full package, stutter included.

While still in the early stages of formation, things were finally beginning to feel right. While I still did not fully understand why I had been given this particular challenge, I did understand that there was meaning and purpose behind it.

But it was more than that. My renewed vigor and fresh outlook were not solely due to my newfound ability to speak in front of an audience. That was a big part of it. However, the underlying feeling ran much deeper than that.

> *I realized that the quest I had begun in order to discover meaning, purpose, and true happiness had value, not just to my individual journey, but also to countless other people searching for meaning and purpose.*

I realized that the quest I had begun in order to discover meaning, purpose, and true happiness had value, not just to my individual journey, but also to countless other people searching for meaning and purpose. For the first time in my life, I was inspiring a wave of young Jews about their rich heritage, something I could only dream of in the past.

There I was, at nineteen years old, teaching Torah to unaffiliated Jews halfway around the world. Also, I was not simply repeating words of Torah I had learned from others, but my classes incorporated my insights, based on years of searching for genuine answers. This included the purpose of the world, man's role in G-d's master plan, prayer, understanding challenges, and also deep textual analysis. Ideas I had learned in Ohr Somayach and Waterbury were now invaluable, not just to me, but also to others who had not been privileged to have such an education.

Moreover, inasmuch as content was helpful, what truly was giving me the ability to inspire others in my new educational efforts, I was told, was my infectious passion for G-d, His Torah, and the Jewish People. At an age when many of my high school peers weren't overly serious about their religious growth, I was trailblazing a path that would never have been possible without my diligent search for the truth, a search that was definitely triggered by my challenges.

FULL-TIME JOB OFFER

Toward the end of my seven-week volunteer stint in Germany, Rabbi Josh Spinner, CEO of the Ronald S. Lauder Foundation, called me into his office. "Thank you for joining us" was all I thought he would say. But to my surprise, he continued.

He proceeded to offer me a one-year, full-time managerial position as Outreach Director for Northern Germany!

I was shocked. While I recognized that I was helpful during my seven-week stint, I never imagined that they would offer me a job, let alone a role that came with much independence and responsibility.

Did they really think that someone with a stutter was the man for the job?!

In addition, not only was I young (not yet twenty years old), but I barely spoke a word of German. Lastly, the position would entail numerous speaking-related responsibilities, including delivering large-scale lectures and developing important relationships with key stakeholders (such as community leaders and philanthropists). Did they really think that someone with a stutter was the man for the job?!

Indeed, I could return to North America, finish university, and find a more standard type of job, but the thought of moving to Europe for a year to help build a sustainable Jewish community was intriguing and unique. It seemed exciting. Would I ever have another opportunity to live abroad and entirely invest myself in communal work?

Moreover, a spark had ignited within me during my brief volunteer stint in Germany. There was a certain sense of comfort and self-confidence I had developed in terms of my stuttering, which finally gave me the courage to not only jump into new social situations, but also to speak in public. For too many years I had felt stifled and inhibited. Seven weeks into my trip to Germany, however, it felt as though I was breaking out of my shell. I became proud enough to accept myself for who I was, stutter included, and to project that persona in social situations.

There was something so liberating about standing up in front of an audience and making a slight joke about my stutter before beginning my speech. It felt healthy. Where had I been all these years? Why hadn't I implemented this tactic up until that point?

I liked it and I wanted more. In a young, idealistic way, I wanted to impact the world. Moreover, in terms of my stuttering, I wanted to transform what was a seven-week experience into my everyday life.

The strategic choice was clear. I accepted the job offer. And two months later, upon completing my undergraduate studies at university, I found myself on a plane to Hamburg, Germany, my new home, as I became the Ronald S. Lauder Foundation's Outreach Director for Northern Germany.

6

TO EUROPE AND BEYOND

Life begins at the end of your comfort zone.

— Neale Donald Walsch

I WAS ON A roll and I loved it.

A one-month immersion course helped me learn some German and navigate the German culture. Meanwhile, I was responsible for building a sustainable educational infrastructure in Northern Germany, where most of the Jews living in the region had recently emigrated from the former Soviet Union. It was a challenging task, as the majority of Jews, through no fault of their own, had very little, if any, understanding of Judaism. Stifled by Communism and shattered by Nazism, Judaism had become a relic, something of the past. Having emigrated from the former Soviet Union to Germany, the local Jewish youth recognized that Judaism was not necessarily the popular thing to practice. And as immigrants, exploring their heritage would certainly put them at an even bigger disadvantage when it came to blending in with the population at large.

That's where I came in. A typical week entailed traveling to numerous cities in northern Germany to teach classes to Jewish youth, organizing social events, and helping prepare large-scale seminars across Europe. Before long, I found myself interfacing with a local member of parliament, a philanthropist, and hundreds of teenagers and young adults who were eager to learn about their heritage.

Remember, please, that less than one year prior to moving to Hamburg, I could barely get my name out when introducing myself in my public speaking course in university. How intoxicating it was, then, that I was thousands of miles away from there, physically and mentally, using my speech as my greatest asset! To this day, I find it mind-boggling.

Remember, please, that less than one year prior to moving to Hamburg, I could barely get my name out when introducing myself in my public speaking course in university.

To effectively communicate, I made my stutter a topic of conversation. There was no longer the proverbial "elephant in the room"; no longer could anxious thoughts and worries play tricks on me. My colleagues knew I stuttered — it was no surprise. Therefore, I was finally able to begin channeling all that head space into the *what* and *how* of what I was presenting, rather than the "Oh no, I'm about to stutter!" train of thought that often plagues those who stutter.

In addition, I discovered that by opening up and becoming vulnerable at the beginning of a meeting, speech, or class, others responded in kind by opening up as well. It is one of the most important pieces of advice that I intend to impart through this book.

After becoming comfortable with who we are, we begin to exude a healthy dose of self-confidence — whether while on a date or at a business meeting or social gathering. People are attracted to that. After all, if we accept ourselves, it only follows that others will accept us too.

Without fail, every person in this world is faced with challenges. Many people, however, are searching for ways to understand, accept, and grow through their unique difficulties. Just because people do not advertise their struggles, it does not mean that they do not exist.

Therefore, I discovered that just by making a little joke about my stutter, I often garner the immediate respect of those with whom I am interacting. I become more relatable to others, still without baring my soul. After all, my stutter would almost certainly come up during a conversation anyway.

Even if just on a practical level, it makes so much sense to let those we are talking to know what to expect; otherwise, at the very least, there is bound to be some awkwardness.

Continuing to incorporate this new strategy, I was on a roll. Over the course of my year in Germany, I frequently taught smaller classes and occasionally delivered larger lectures. I felt happier about myself; I felt proud for not shying away from circumstances. I felt like I was finally becoming the person I was meant to be.

CREATOR AND SUSTAINER

In my ensuing interaction with hundreds of Jewish youth, I discovered a critical philosophical gap that needed to be filled. Many of them honestly believed that G-d created the world. However, they did not truly recognize that He is intimately involved with every aspect of our lives.

The following story illustrates one such example:

> During a program we organized in the picturesque Swiss Alps, I was asked to speak to one of the participants who was being highly disruptive.
>
> Our conversation quickly evolved into a philosophical debate. "Prove to me that G-d exists," she stated.
>
> "Prove to me that G-d exists," she stated.
>
> I began to compile a mental list of "proofs" that I thought might satisfy her, but then I quickly realized that her request was not asked in question form; rather, it was a challenge. It occurred to me that she knew very well that G-d existed and she needed no further proof of that. She had attended Jewish schools and this had been ingrained in her since childhood. Clearly, she was ready to deflect any proof I would offer, as she had probably done countless times with previous teachers. As such, any intellectual response would be totally futile.

My response, therefore, took on a style like it never had before. At that moment, it seemed crystal clear that it was what she needed to hear. (And because I had never responded like that before, it felt as though G-d was putting the perfect words into my mouth.)

"Is it all right with you if we try to rephrase your question, which would help us get to the core of what is truly bothering you?"

"Sure," she answered, somewhat skeptically.

"You were born in Israel; you grew up with miracles taking place all around you. You know deep down that G-d created you, takes care of you, and loves you. There is no doubt in your mind of that being 100 percent reality. What's troubling you, however, is how to piece it all together. If He loves you so much, why has He made your life so challenging? You're so young; what did you ever do wrong? Why does your family dynamic have to be so complicated and difficult? Couldn't He just put you in a "normal" family? After all, doesn't He want you to just be happy?"

The ensuing silence was palpable. It seemed like this revelation penetrated an inner part of her where nobody else had ventured before. Perhaps she had not even consciously understood her own questions.

Thirty seconds (which seemed like an eternity) later, she looked up, teary eyed. "Yes, you are right. That is what I am truly asking..."

"It's very mature of you to recognize that. We just accomplished a tremendous feat. We no longer have this *ambiguity to your belief in G-d. It is as firm as ever. And because it is, because you know that He exists and is intimately involved with your life, you are baffled as to why He has made things so difficult for you.*

"Before trying to answer that question, though, let's spend a day or two digesting this new development. Afterward, then, we can begin to try to wrap our heads around the concept of why G-d challenges those He loves."

RAISON D'ÊTRE

Based on this interaction (and many others like it), I realized how much more we all could gain if we only inculcated and truly lived by these ideals.

After spending years delving into Judaism's approach to these philosophical questions (because of the challenges I had been going through), it was now time to "pay it forward," to spread these timeless Torah messages to those who weren't as fortunate to receive such educational opportunities and experiences. As such, sharing these insights became my raison d'être throughout my time in Germany and beyond.

Yet it wasn't just a matter of engaging in theological discussions. It was also the way in which I did so. While I was growing up, I viewed Judaism — or any other religion for that matter — as archaic, irrelevant for a modern, twenty-first century lifestyle. And it seemed like many others shared that perspective. But through my education and interaction with religious role models, I discovered how much beauty, meaning, and true happiness could be found within that framework.

Therefore, it was truly a privilege to share my knowledge and experiences with others — in an upbeat and fun way.

Our Passover Seder in Hamburg was one such example of spreading that message. About sixty participants showed up for what turned out to be a monumental night. The room was packed with Jews from diverse backgrounds: Germans, Russians, North Americans, and Israelis (soldiers temporarily in Germany to be trained by the German Navy, who showed up at the synagogue looking for a Seder).

The two main themes we stressed were: 1) Feeling as if *we* left Egypt, recognizing the relevance of personal bondage and "freeing" ourselves from it by recognizing G-d's loving hand behind it all; and 2) experiencing true joy, as a natural outgrowth of it.

With matzah-themed beach balls, puppet shows for the Ten Plagues, and Haggadah (Passover-specific text) insights being shared in numerous languages (including a special Chinese rendition of one of the popular songs), it was an incredibly moving experience.

The Seder was going strong well past midnight, and at about two o'clock in the morning, the German police came to check on a noise complaint. What a sight it must have been for them to see such a diverse group of Jews celebrating Passover in Germany once again!

Feedback was so positive. People had never experienced anything like it.

Whether for the Israeli soldiers, who often have a "been there, done that" attitude after having grown up surrounded by Israeli culture, or the Russian/German Jews, who felt that Judaism was outdated, Judaism came alive in unprecedented ways for all of them. Passover was infused with much depth, meaning, and relevance. It became exciting and beautiful. And ultimately, having a meaningful relationship with G-d finally seemed possible.

It was new and special for me, as well. No longer angry with G-d, I knew, deep down, that He really loved me and was guiding me through life — the very message of Passover itself. And I was beginning to catch more of a glimpse into the purposes behind my challenges — for I never would have been running such educational programs in Germany at such a young age, had I not experienced difficulties growing up.

> No longer angry with G-d, I knew, deep down, that He really loved me and was guiding me through life — the very message of Passover itself.

There was a lot more to do. Life was busy, and at times exhausting. (During the Intermediary Days of Passover, I flew to Italy to teach at a seminar in Tuscany.) Yet the more I felt empowered by the message I was imparting (and recognizing that it was having its desired effect), the more energy and enthusiasm I felt as I went forward. This was coupled with a deep sense of genuine happiness and satisfaction in being able to channel my interests, talent, and life experiences into helping others lead more meaningful and happy lives.

BACK IN TORONTO

Although I was asked to continue working in Germany beyond my one-year contract, I decided to return to Toronto instead, where I began to work in business. It had been my goal to be rooted in business (as a career), yet still devote considerable time and energy to Jewish education. It was clearly my passion, and I was coming to realize that it was also, at least in part, my calling. Upon returning to Toronto, I was enthusiastic about continuing my efforts to impact the community around me. So, in addition to traveling back to Germany on a number of occasions to continue helping with their programs (which included a newly formed leadership training program), I began to teach a weekly philosophy course to high school seniors enrolled in Torah High, an enriching, extra-curricular program for public school students, organized through the National Conference of Synagogue Youth (NCSY).

The class was a new experience for me, as I was neither accustomed to teaching in formal settings nor for high school credit. Teachers were required to give students assignments, tests, and a final exam, all the things which I hoped not to do, so as not to ruin my ability to inspire the students. I was determined nevertheless to design creative, thought-provoking solutions that would fit the curriculum requirements.

One of my favorite assignments was the one on challenges. During a three-part series I taught on embracing our unique challenges, I assigned the students the following task: Choose a challenge that you, or someone close to you, experienced in the past. Now, reflecting back on it, explain how something positive evolved from that very challenge.

> *Honestly, I was not expecting much depth from my students. They were young. And it seemed like all they were interested in were college applications, their upcoming prom, and how to get a high school credit without doing much work.*

Honestly, I was not expecting much depth from my students. They were young. And it seemed like all they were interested in were college applications, their upcoming prom, and how to get a high school credit without doing much work. So their responses totally floored me; some brought tears to my eyes. Each wrote about a personal difficulty, and something positive that evolved from it.

For instance, one student wrote about his uncle, whom he described as a workaholic, who was diagnosed with cancer. The experience for his entire family was frightening and challenging, as it made the future very uncertain for them.

Reflecting back, however, he described it as the best thing that could have happened. Not only did his uncle recover, but with his newfound health and appreciation for life and family, his uncle now also carves out sacred dedicated family time each week, so as not to squander away the precious opportunity to be with them.

Another student wrote about her sister's struggle with severe emotional issues which manifested in dramatic outbursts in her home. She too described how it ultimately brought her family closer together.

Many of the students had come from upper-class families, and gave the impression that everything was blissful and perfect. But through this project, I came to recognize their true depth and emotional capabilities. Together, the students and I understood that everyone goes through his own unique challenges. And while some challenges are more apparent than others (such as stuttering), we are each given unique opportunities to grow and gain a closer relationship with G-d.

The purpose of my assignment, therefore, was to introduce them to the idea that even though we often cannot see any possible good coming from a difficult situation when we are going through it, we can often see, in hindsight, how it was beneficial in some way. As a continuation of this, when concluding the three-part series, I asked my students to try to remember to view their current and future challenges as loving gifts from G-d, because that would enable them to gain a significantly deeper and more meaningful relationship with Him.

THE SILVER LINING OF STUTTERING

This powerful experience encouraged me to take an even closer look at my stuttering. How did it enhance my life? What positive takeaways were there from that which caused me so much agony?

I wasn't finished stuttering. It wasn't just a "challenge from the past," like the assignment I gave to my students; my stutter posed ongoing difficulties. While I had become more self-confident — I could express myself better and I was becoming more resilient — I still continued to struggle with it. My stuttering was an issue in various settings, including at work.

For instance, someone contacted the CEO of a multibillion dollar cosmetics company and requested that he get in touch with me to discuss collaboration opportunities. I was told that he had my office number and would call me to follow up.

My boss was enthusiastic about the possibilities... but I was freaking out about my stutter.

Could this be the big break of my career? I wondered. *If, during my short call with the CEO, I could convince him to partner with my company, my trajectory would be quite promising. Would I be given the lead role on this new unprecedented strategic partnership?*

My boss was enthusiastic about the possibilities...but I was freaking out about my stutter.

Notwithstanding all the positive psychology I had taught myself, philosophical insights into the reasons for challenges, and the new mechanisms I had created to decrease anxiety in this exact situation, it felt almost impossible to remain calm. Compounding my anxiety was the fact that I shared office space with two other employees in the company. I thought, *Even if I stutter over the phone and the CEO is patient and kind enough to understand, how will my colleagues respond, knowing that I may be squandering the opportunity of a lifetime?*

None of this had any basis, because my colleagues already knew that I stuttered and they were fine with it. Nobody expected me to come across as a smooth-talking salesman during my call; rather, they were appreciative that I extended myself in the first place, regardless of the outcome. However, in my mind, I had built up an imaginary world of unhealthy and unhelpful anxiety.

I can still recall the way I was gripped with fear. For those couple of days while I awaited his call, I felt debilitated. *What if...? What if...? What if...?* I remember hoping that the call would come through when my colleagues were out to lunch or on an extended bathroom break. I remember those days being very unproductive altogether.

And it felt terrible. *Wasn't I too old for this? Didn't I already break loose of this seemingly immature behavioral pattern? Couldn't I just, once and for all, leave the stuttering behind me?*

It is important to note that, at around this time, I was periodically traveling back and forth to Europe to continue teaching for the Ronald S. Lauder Foundation. In addition, I was invited to teach at a youth leadership program in Sydney, Australia, where I lectured, once again with enthusiasm and confidence, in front of six hundred high school students.

I realized, therefore, that while my speech-related confidence had exponentially improved, I was not quite "there" yet. I still had more work to do with respect to the anxiety surrounding my stuttering. Indeed, I had already come so far, further than I could have imagined. But I still needed to look ahead. What areas still needed improvement? How could I confidently assert myself during a business meeting, without feeling crippled by my stutter? Why couldn't I leverage my "success" in all other areas?

As such, the assignment in my Torah High class was relevant for me too. What did I glean from all these years of stuttering? How could I continue to stay positive about it, notwithstanding continued episodes where it would still impede my ability to fully express myself?

> *It is important to note that it wasn't about not stuttering; rather, it was about feeling comfortable with my stutter.*

It is important to note that it wasn't about not stuttering; rather, it was about feeling comfortable with my stutter. I should have been able to calmly inform the CEO, right at the beginning of our call, that I stuttered, just like I had countless times before in different scenarios, including lectures to large audiences. What was so dramatically different about this particular situation?

Clearly, not only were my Torah High students in need of my adversity-related assignment, but I was too, as a reminder of the ultimate benefits of my challenging experiences as a person who stutters.

HOW STUTTERING CHANGED ME

Four specific character traits, in my particular case, began to emerge as a result of the years of pain and anger that were rooted in my years of stuttering. (As you read through this section, feel free to allow your thoughts to wander and focus on those areas in which you, too, recognize the growth that can stem from your unique challenges.)

Sensitivity

I will begin with sensitivity. If you do not stutter, it is nearly impossible to really understand what it means to do so. You simply cannot comprehend what it is like to be totally and completely unable to get a word out of your mouth.

There are actually three variations of stuttering-related disfluencies:

Blocks — Mouth opens but nothing comes out; the words get "stuck."

Repetitions — Sound or word gets repeated numerous times.

Prolongations — First sound gets stretched.

As you read through this section, feel free to allow your thoughts to wander and focus on those areas in which you, too, recognize the growth that can stem from your unique challenges.

None of the above are pleasant. They can be awkward for all parties involved. For the listener, he may have no idea what to do. If he knows what the stutterer is trying to say, should he assist him in getting the word out? Should he avert his eyes or maintain contact? What about offering suggestions, such as "Why don't you take a deep breath and try again"? (See appendix 1 for advice on what to do in these situations.)

For the one who is stuttering, it is uncomfortable, awkward, and painful. It is outright embarrassing. I know this from many firsthand situations. I grew up being laughed at. Not only was I the brunt of jokes, but I was also laughed at just because people did not know how else to respond. (By the way, please note that this happens till this very day. For instance, if I stutter on my name, people sarcastically, yet often innocently, ask, "Did you forget your name?!" I don't blame them; they are simply trying to break the ice, to make light of an otherwise awkward situation.)

Sensitivity. As I mentioned before, if you don't stutter, you cannot even imagine what it is like to be unable to speak. Similarly, I learned, since I do not have a lisp, I cannot imagine what it is like to be unable to properly pronounce the letter *s*.

Taking it a little further, even though I could not understand why some classmates couldn't properly shoot a basketball, I was able to stretch my sensitivity to include scenarios that I couldn't understand about other people, such as their being bad at sports. How I could I ever make fun of them? Having been on the receiving end of laughs, there was no way I would ever make someone feel the way I felt when I was taunted.

But it goes much further than that. With my experience as the victim, not only would I avoid shaming anyone, but I would also actively try to help others in areas in which I was more fortunate. That may have meant helping a classmate with his math homework by patiently reciting the multiplication or division tables again and again. I would constantly remind myself: Just like I sometimes cannot get words out of my mouth, he cannot get the math concepts into his head.

During my teenage years, I coached a little league softball team and made an extra effort to be sensitive to the players on my team who were not as skilled as the others. I impressed upon them the importance of mutual respect and playing for fun. It turned out to be a great summer. And I continued to volunteer in many different settings, always trying to patiently and sensitively help others.

Sensitivity takes us a long way. Now, as a parent, I have a much greater appreciation for the famous Jewish adage, penned by the wise King Solomon: "Educate a child according to his way."[16] It is natural for parents to have an agenda for their children, desiring certain schools, grades, sports affiliations, and even professions, regardless of the child's inherent abilities. Parents often feel that these things reflect back on them. As a result, the child's character traits and innate talents may be ignored because parents so badly want to be viewed in a certain way.

"Educate a child according to his way" means that parents need to be sensitive to their children. Parents' agendas should take a back seat to the child's strengths and weaknesses. The child must come first. Yes, I may like my son to be a pitcher for his little league baseball team. But if he does not have the wherewithal to pitch or if he simply wants to do something else instead, that is also okay.

Sensitivity helps us think about other people, putting ourselves in their shoes, recognizing how things may feel for them. People who grow up with challenges often develop a keen sensitivity to others.

Self-Confidence

A second area in which I grew through my stuttering, surprising as it may sound, is self-confidence. Allow me to clarify: There was a fascinating exchange that took place during my month-long intensive speech therapy course. One morning, Lori, the group facilitator, asked the group whether we would prefer to be called "stutterers" or "individuals who stutter." She explained that she was at a wedding the night before and someone asked her what she does. She then found herself hesitating about the answer — *Do I work with "stutterers" or "those who stutter"?* While the question may sound simple, it was

---
16   *Mishlei* 22:6.

actually quite deep. Did those of us in the group that morning feel that we could be classified by our stutter?

Alternatively, did we feel as though we were "individuals with a stutter" — individuals first and with stuttering second? Did we feel as though we were individuals — each of us a person with a unique world surrounding us — and then, part of that world includes a speech impediment called stuttering?

Although this incident took place about a decade ago, it replays vividly in my mind. One girl with a particularly severe stutter responded that she could be referred to as a "stutterer." The heaviness in the room was palpable, without anyone actually being able to pinpoint what that label meant. I, then, spoke up and proudly described who I am — an individual who comes from a large family, loves eating pizza, playing baseball, spending time with friends, and who also has a stutter. But never would I put my stutter in the forefront of my life. Yes, it is a part of me; but no, it does not define me. I wouldn't call myself a "stutterer."[17]

(I recently saw a speech therapist describe his clients — and other individuals who stutter — as "PWS" [people who stutter]. The person does not have to be labeled a "stutterer," because as we mentioned before, there is so much more to a person than the physical way in which his speech manifests. In other words, I'm a person. I'm not a speech-impediment. It is but one of the many features that describe me, but not the defining one.)

My self-confidence materialized substantially as I became a young adult. A major factor in my development was the acceptance of stuttering as part of my package, to be able to confidently include it on the list of what comprises me, Moe Mernick.

---

17   That is why you will rarely, if ever, hear me refer to someone as a "stutterer," even though it is quicker and easier to say than "a person with a stutter."

My stuttering was no longer something to hide or to be embarrassed about. I had to step up to the plate, to show myself I could do it. My conversations with Lori reinforced the idea that it is better to lead a life with a stutter than to lead no life at all. And a life with a stutter, I discovered, could in fact be a truly beautiful life.

Make no mistake. This transformation did not occur overnight. Quite the contrary, the transformation is still taking place. The first few months and years were certainly the most challenging, but I still find myself faced with new scenarios all the time. This is an ongoing part of my life, being able to comfortably assert, toward the beginning of a conversation or public speech, that I have a stutter.

Having a positive attitude regarding our challenges can lead to the development of deep and authentic self-confidence.

In fact, the greatest testament to my developing comfort with my stutter is the fact that I am "going public" about it. To have my name fully associated with stuttering demonstrates that I am becoming confident and comfortable with who I am.

Having a positive attitude regarding our challenges can lead to the development of deep and authentic self-confidence.

Appreciation

Please take a few moments to think about the following:

When was the last time you thought about your ability to walk, to take a stroll through a beautiful park, or to run to catch a bus?

When was the last time you thought about your ability to see, to enjoy a gorgeous sunset?

When was the last time you thought about your ability to smell, to appreciate the delicious aroma of hot chocolate, or the smell of roses?

When was the last time you thought about your ability to speak, to introduce yourself to someone new, or make casual conversation with the cashier in a store?

For each of these scenarios, the one who is lacking the ability — either walking, seeing, smelling, or speaking — definitely thinks about it often.

Deaf and blind, Helen Keller penned a highly acclaimed poem in which she described what her exact itinerary would be if she was granted temporary eyesight. She summarized the poem, "Three Days to See," with the following powerful paragraph:

> *I who am blind can give one hint to those who see — one admonition to those who would make full use of the gift of sight: Use your eyes as if tomorrow you would be stricken blind. And the same method can be applied to the other senses. Hear the music of voices, the song of a bird, the mighty strains of an orchestra, as if you would be stricken deaf tomorrow. Touch each object you want to touch as if tomorrow your tactile sense would fail. Smell the perfume of flowers, taste with relish each morsel, as if tomorrow you could never smell and taste again. Make the most of every sense; glory in all the facets of pleasure and beauty which the world reveals to you through the several means of contact which nature provides. But of all the senses, I am sure that sight must be the most delightful.*

How often do we appreciate what we have? Regrettably, it is natural for us to focus on what we do not have. Simple research into the basic workings of any body part would have us absolutely dumbfounded. Too often, though, we find ourselves dreaming of the newest electronic gadget or exotic vacation rather than recognizing the myriad blessings in our lives.

If a person becomes deathly ill, his entire life revolves around trying to get better; if a person loses his ability to walk following a car accident, he focuses entirely on physiotherapy to regain that ability. In Helen Keller's case, she dreamed about sight — a sense which many of us may have never even appreciated.

One of my father-in-law's favorite quotes echoes this sentiment: "Success is getting what you want; happiness is wanting what you get." To be satisfied with what we have makes us the wealthiest people in the world. As the famous Jewish adage states: "Who is rich? One who is happy with what he has."[18]

Tony Robbins, one of the most popular motivational speakers of our generation, agrees. During one of his lectures, in which he boasted that he knows the secret to success and happiness, he prescribed that we should all begin our day by expressing gratitude.

For those who do not stutter, why not show some appreciation for the ability to speak fluently (thereby avoiding the pain, embarrassment, and frustration that I described in the earlier chapters)? For those of us who do stutter, when was the last time we expressed appreciation for our ability to see, hear, or walk?

We previously discussed Art Berg, who became paralyzed from the waist down. When was the last time we showed appreciation for the fact that we can move both of our feet?

---

18   *Pirkei Avot* 4:1.

For all of us, when was the last time we woke up in the morning and sincerely thanked our parents/spouse/siblings/children for being in our lives, appreciated the school/job that we have, enthusiastically thanked the mailman for delivering the mail, garbage man for picking up our trash, and bus driver for arriving on time? Appreciating the "simple" things in life can enable us to feel blessed beyond words.

Therefore, whether through affirmations or prayer, let us begin each day on the right foot; let us recognize the gifts that we take for granted. Instead of focusing on what is beyond us, let us rejoice for what is within our grasp.

And let us also learn from the incredible example of Sorale Krigsman, who recently passed away after a long struggle with cancer. Her husband spoke at her funeral and shared that when his wife was first diagnosed, she decided that she did not want the disease to take over her or her family's lives. She kept things a secret from her young children and put her best foot forward every day while battling, struggling, and dealing with a lot of pain.

Finally her doctor told her that she did not have much more time. She decided that she was going to tell her youngest son, who was thirteen years old at the time.

When the boy came home from camp at the end of the summer, he could immediately tell something was wrong. His mother proceeded to explain. Her son's response was simple, innocent, and powerful.

"Why you?"

Sorale had always been a model mother and citizen, a giver, a powerful and positive force in her community and in the world. The question, therefore, was very real. Why?

We should take a lesson from her answer.

> When I first started dating and immediately found the love of my life, I didn't ask, Why me? When I became pregnant in the first year of marriage, when so many of our friends struggled for years to conceive, I didn't ask, Why me? When I was fortunate enough to never struggle financially, as my husband was blessed with making a good living, I didn't ask, Why me? When my older children got married with ease and started their own beautiful families, I didn't ask, Why me? So I'm not going to start asking now.

With the right proactive and positive attitude, our adversity can lead to a deep sense of appreciation for the many good things in our lives.

Zest for Life

"How are you?" is perhaps the most frequently asked question around. This pleasantry has become such a social formality that it has practically turned into a statement. By this, I am remembering the countless times I was asked the question, but the person moved away before I had the chance to answer.

"Wait!" I call out, somewhat confused. But my questioner's back is turned to me as he continues on his way, forgetting that he just asked me a question. "Weren't you wondering how I'm doing?!"

Nevertheless, when people actually respond to this, in my experience it is usually with one of the three following responses:

1. Good.
2. Not bad.
3. Can't complain.

Let's focus on the second one for a moment — "not bad."

"Not bad"?! Does he mean that "bad" is the usual, but today, well, lo and behold, he's "not bad"? His job is in place, his wife loves him, and the sun is shining. Hmmm...time to celebrate. He's NOT bad!

It gets better, though, because my least favorite response is "can't complain." Usually, this guy complains (or at least it seems like he does from the words he uses). Today, however, though he wants to complain, everything seems to be going just right! He slept through the night, he had a spectacular morning coffee, and there was no traffic on the way to work. His boss was in a good mood and even complimented him on his most recent project!

Oh man, can't complain about that today!

Oh man, can't complain about *that* today! His wife cooked a delicious dinner and his kids actually said "I love you, Dad" before going to sleep at night. Can't complain there either...

Is that what life has come to? If everything is going so well, why can't we express that goodness?

Frankly, I can cut some slack for the guy who responds with "good," because even though it usually lacks enthusiasm, at least it is not as negative-sounding as the others.

But really, where is our zest for life? If we have learned from this book that "life is beautiful," then why aren't we responding with a resounding "life is beautiful!"?

I have given this a lot of thought. How many times have I been asked the question, only to give a halfhearted, pessimistic response? Granted, one may say that those three responses — "good," "not bad," and "can't complain" — are the norm, and people will look at you strangely if you respond with more enthusiasm.

Do you know what? You may be right!

Several years ago, I was flying from Tel Aviv to New York and had a stopover in Berlin. After landing in Berlin at about five-thirty in the morning (after very little sleep, if any), I headed straight to Tegel Airport's Starbucks for a caffeine boost and a comfortable couch. While taking my order, the barista politely asked, "How are you?" To which I responded, "*Ausgezeichnet* (German for 'amazing')! I just had an incredible trip to Israel and I am excited to return to New York. But in addition to that, there is no Starbucks in Israel and I am therefore SO excited to have one of your coffees again!"

The barista, who was obviously still waking up at that early hour, seemed somewhat taken aback. "I have never heard anyone answer like that before. Choose any drink you want — absolutely free!"

To quote one sentence from Wikipedia's lengthy, yet intriguing definition of the word "zest": "Zest is a positive trait reflecting a person's approach to life with anticipation, energy, enthusiasm, and excitement."

Just like in a game of poker, we do not choose the hand we are dealt, but we are in control of the way we play our cards. So, too, in life, we have two choices: sulk about our hardships, excusing ourselves for not becoming great, or view our struggles as unique opportunities to affect the world, using them as vehicles for true greatness.

"Zest is a positive trait reflecting a person's approach to life with anticipation, energy, enthusiasm, and excitement."

There was a lot of positivity that resulted from my stutter. And, therefore, feeling empowered because I chose the latter of the two aforementioned options, I was consciously leading my life with true zest — "anticipation, energy, enthusiasm, and excitement."

NEXT STEPS

Focusing on the ways in which I have grown through my stuttering helped a lot. It helped me deepen my appreciation for the person I have become, which was clearly only possible due to the challenges I faced.

Strengthened by this notion, I kicked it up a notch, spending the next couple of years continuing to teach in different settings around the world, growing spiritually, and being truly happy with myself.

At this point, another big test was coming. I was ready to look for my life partner. How would my stutter play a role in that?

7

DATING, MARRIAGE, AND FAMILY

> *Forty days before the creation of a child, a Heavenly voice proclaims "the daughter of this person (will be married) to this one."*
>
> — *Talmud*[19]

THE FOLLOWING STORY occurred during the final revisions of this book. Its direct relevance to this chapter made it apropos to include as a segue into my personal journey through dating and marriage.

---

19 *Sotah* 2a.

On Friday morning, shortly after Passover, a nineteen-year-old Chassidic (ultra-Orthodox) boy traveled with both of his parents from Rockland County to Riverdale, New York to visit his speech therapist, Dr. Phil Schneider, a leading specialist in stuttering.

"Doc, how do you think he's doing?" the parents asked immediately after arriving at Dr. Schneider's office.

"I haven't seen him since before Passover, so I'm not really sure." Dr. Schneider then turned to the young man and asked, "How do *you* think you're doing?"

"I am doing well," he sheepishly responded.

Dr. Schneider wondered whether there was more to the parents' question. But he didn't have to wait for long, because they jumped in with their second question. "Doc, do you think he's ready?"

"Ready…for what?"

"Well, ready for *shidduchim* (dating for marriage)."

"With all due respect, I am a speech therapist. I know a lot about stuttering and a few other things, but matchmaking is not one of them."

"We weren't in a rush for him to start dating, but we were called about a wonderful girl who may be suitable. They say that everything about her is perfect; she is a very desirable match. But they also say she rejects everyone she meets. This one for this reason, that one for another reason. And they say she is so picky that she is waiting for her Moshe Rabbeinu (Moses) to walk through the door!"

"Sounds perfect!" exclaimed Dr. Schneider. "Your son has a stutter and she is waiting for her Moshe Rabbeinu, who also stuttered; it is a match made in Heaven!"

"But he stutters; what do you think will be?" the parents nervously asked.

Turning again to the boy, Dr. Schneider warmly questioned him, "Do you have a stutter?"

"Yes."

"Do you want to be married to a girl who couldn't tolerate that you stutter?"

"No."

"So when you meet her, why not tell her that you stutter?"

"Really? You think so?" The boy seemed puzzled.

"You don't want to be married to her anyway if she doesn't accept you. If she's looking for someone perfect, you might as well tell her right away. Especially if you and your family feel comfortable about it, I don't think it's a bad idea to put it on the table."

Shortly thereafter, the young man called Dr. Schneider, something he had never done before.

"Mazel tov…I'm engaged!"

He went on to explain that he took the idea, as crazy as it sounded, and was open with this girl about his stuttering on their first date. Apparently, she found it endearing and attractive for him to be so up front about something that some considered to be an imperfection.

That, then, made him the perfect match for her.

MY NOTEBOOK

On my bookshelf, proudly displayed with my other *sefarim* (traditional Jewish texts), is a small notebook from my time in Israel. It includes my Gemara (Talmud) and *parshah* (weekly Torah portion) notes, as well as some of my earliest recorded Torah insights.

What makes it most unique, though, is that it also includes an invaluable assignment I was given during my time at Ohr Somayach:

to project into my life ahead. What were my short-term and long-term goals? What kind of girl did I want to marry? What kind of home did I want to build?

I remember the feeling of describing the type of girl with whom I wanted to build a home and raise a family. I dreamed big. Yet at the same time, I was nervous. *Would that kind of girl want to marry me? Wouldn't someone with all those wonderful traits I valued want someone who could speak fluently? Would she stand confidently by my side during the stuttering episodes that would inevitably occur? Why would she unnecessarily want to complicate her life?* These thoughts troubled me.

Yet, as a result of my personal growth over the years, those feelings almost completely dissipated when I was ready to start dating. I was looking forward to this new exciting stage of life. I truly felt that G-d had a special girl for me, who would be comfortable with my stutter. After all, G-d gave me the stutter; I did not ask for it. Therefore, in His infinite wisdom, He would also have a special young woman for me who was not just okay with it, but also appreciated the person I became *because* of it.

After all, G-d gave me the stutter; I did not ask for it. Therefore, in His infinite wisdom, He would also have a special young woman for me who was not just okay with it, but also appreciated the person I became **because** *of it.*

My future-wife, Melanie, heard about my stutter just a few days before we were to meet. And at first, she was nervous — not for herself, but for me. *How embarrassing it must be to stutter in public,* she thought. *What gives him the strength to continue to speak in front of others? How does he manage to maintain a positive attitude toward something so inherently challenging?*

As we dated, my wife got to know me for who I was: an individual who had become comfortable with his stutter and had grown through his challenges. She appreciated my openness on the subject, the way I confidently handled myself during stuttering episodes, and my positivity throughout. We had a lot of fun together and connected deeply on shared goals for our future.

Several months later, we were engaged. Mazel tov!

THE SHABBAT BEFORE MY WEDDING

Then, an unbelievable story occurred. It was by far the most anxiety-ridden, stutter-related incident of my engagement: the Shabbat before the wedding, when I was to be called to the Torah and subsequently read the *Haftarah* (a passage from the Prophetic writings) before the congregation. Surprising as it may be, the *Haftarah* was the easy part (because of its accompanying melody and the fact that one does not stutter when singing, as previously explained); the simple *aliyah* (when I would be called up to recite the accompanying blessings) however, was a tremendous source of stress.

I was very nervous. I felt like I was having heart palpitations. And rightfully so: My fiancé's father and grandfather were standing nearby, and I really hoped not to dampen the festive mood by creating a full-out public display of my stutter. My Hebrew name was then joyfully sung, indicating that it was my turn at the Torah. Everyone looked on with enthusiasm, without a clue as to my enormous fear; inside, I was freaking out.

Silently begging G-d for His help, I sheepishly approached the platform where the Torah was being read, donned a prayer shawl, and looked at the part of the Torah scroll where the reader would begin. While directing me to the right place, the reader also whispered the first few words he was about to read.

I couldn't believe what they were:

"*Vayomer Hashem el Moshe: Al tira* (And G-d said to Moshe: Do not fear)."[20]

Tears welled up in my eyes. I was blown away. It felt like a prophetic message, like G-d was clearly speaking to me.

With my wedding around the corner and an extremely stressful situation upon me, He relayed to me a poignant message, through His timeless Torah: "Moshe (Moe), there is no need to fear. I am with you all the way. I gave you your stutter, and I will help you get through this."

> "Moshe (Moe), there is no need to fear. I am with you all the way. I gave you your stutter, and I will help you get through this."

Those words stick with me to this day. Whether in a particularly stressful situation or not, I remind myself not only of the powerful words, *al tira* (do not fear), but also of the words the Torah used to preface that remark — *Vayomer Hashem el Moshe* (And G-d said to Moshe). G-d spoke to me. He knows that I exist. He cares about me. And everything He does is for the best.

Clear messages like that are not daily occurrences. But on the cusp of my wedding, it was a powerful message to internalize. Regardless of the circumstance, He was, is, and will continue to be there with me — and, therefore, there is no need to fear.

---

20 *Bamidbar* 21:34.

MELANIE'S VIEW

You may also enjoy hearing about my dating experience from my wife, Melanie:

Moshe and I were suggested to each other long before we actually met. It took several years for us to be in the same place at the same time, considering that first I had to finish high school! Everything I heard about Moshe from my high school teacher, who was also a mutual friend, was charming and exciting. Around the time the suggestion came up in a more formal manner, Moshe had just returned from a year of living and teaching in Germany, was on his way to Australia for the summer to run Jewish outreach programming, and then would be heading back home to "settle down." Hearing about his independence, inner strength, passion for Judaism, and love of teaching and traveling (to name a few of his good points), I was psyched and could only imagine that Moshe was all I was looking for. My parents, being more conservative in nature, knew about this fantasy of mine but gently tried to push things off year after year. Finally, while we were both spending time back in Israel, our first date happened. And as they say, the rest is history. Thank G-d!

Before dating, I knew that Moshe had gone through some rough patches (i.e., his parents' divorce, leaving high school early), and although it may seem strange, I admired him more because of it all. Knowing the kind of person he was and where he was holding in life made my respect for him grow tremendously, even before I knew what he looked like! And, in the same vein, hearing about Moshe's enthusiasm and energy really impressed me.

Everyone knows how to enjoy and appreciate the good times; I wanted to know that the person I would marry would be someone with whom I could work through, and even more so, grow with through the inevitable hard times, as well. Someone who can grow through the challenges sent his way and yet continue to develop and inspire himself and others — that is someone I want to learn from and raise a family with.

> Everyone knows how to enjoy and appreciate the good times; I wanted to know that the person I would marry would be someone with whom I could work through, and even more so, grow with through the inevitable hard times, as well.

Now, remember this is all BEFORE Moshe and I actually dated. How does this all relate to his stutter? Precisely the point — it doesn't! I did not know, until just a couple of days before I met him, that Moshe stuttered. It didn't come up in any conversations about him and it never crossed my mind that something could be "wrong" with him. For a brief moment, I may have felt a bit slighted — how could someone forget to mention this important, potentially awkward, point? But that feeling only came from a sense of "I don't want to make him uncomfortable. What do I do when he stutters? Will he want to talk about it?" Needless to say, now that you have read most of this book and you know the kind of person he is, our first date, and each one thereafter, was smooth and beautiful. When I recall our dating, I don't at all think of awkward moments and uncomfortable conversations. This was the man of my dreams, he was perfect for me in every way. And he had a stutter.

It was on our third date, in the heart of Jerusalem, when Moshe really opened up to me about his stutter. I don't recall much of the actual conversation, but I clearly remember my feelings as he spoke, which I still often feel when Moshe is saying a Torah thought at family occasions or teaching a class to a large audience: *How is he doing this? He is so unbelievably brave!*

One evening, when we were already dating seriously, I was reading through my notes from a class I attended on the topic of dating and marriage. One of the most practical and powerful points I remember till this day, and often relate to my students and siblings, is: *Ask yourself, Am I proud to introduce this person to anyone and everyone I know?* This is a crucial measure of how you feel about the person you are seeing. I recall feeling guilty as I reviewed the question in my mind, thinking of the few instances that Moshe tried to order food or direct the taxi or say a simple thank-you, and stuttered. But, almost immediately, my thoughts changed to, *Why am I uncomfortable? Moshe is totally proud and confident about who he is. He goes out of his way to speak, whether when he's meeting new people, saying thank-you to everyone, and everything in between.*

And he totally proved me right. The first time Moshe came over to my house and met my extended family, he calmly and comically mentioned, in these words, "I just want to let you know that my stutter might pop up to say hi." What a great way to break the ice.

> *I can never say that I know what it's like to stutter. But I do know what it's like to live with someone who does.*

Many of us can hide our challenges. They are concealed to the world. Stuttering is hard, if not impossible, to hide. I can never say that I know what it's like to stutter. But I do know what it's like to live with someone who does. As Moshe and I are constantly deepening our relationship, I am so much more attuned to the nuances of the world of stuttering. We travel, go out to eat, meet new people, read books to our kids, even run Shabbat programs — all of which can be nightmares for someone who stutters. I am thrilled that, at this point in time, Moshe and I are able to smile at each other after I realize he changed a word in his speech, or wink when he gets through leading the *bentching* (Grace after Meals) without needing to pause. I know that when someone asks my husband his name or age, it may take a few extra seconds and probably a chuckle from the inquirer before he can introduce himself.

I respectfully suggest to *shadchanim* (matchmakers) out there to make sure that a person's stutter is not at the top of the list, weeding people out. I am not proposing the idea of keeping this information hidden until the couple meets, but I am advising that this not be the first point, nor the most emphasized one. (Of course, a potential spouse has to feel comfortable and be accepting, but those things come with time, discussion, and hopefully some laughs).

And to those out there who are too afraid to start dating because of a debilitating stutter, or for that matter, any other physical or emotional challenge, know that there are people who will appreciate you *because* of your struggles and challenges and the person you have become. As the proud wife and number one fan of a man who stutters, I wish everyone reading this, whether you are going through a challenge or supporting someone who is, a deep, enriching, joyous marriage and future.

PARENTING

Soon enough, Melanie and I were blessed with becoming parents. I began to clearly see the striking parallel between the parent/child and G-d/person dynamic, one that is often referred to in our prayers. Perhaps the first time it was crystallized for me was when I was putting my son to sleep when he was about three months old.

He liked when I was in the room with him. Even if I wasn't actually holding him, he instinctively knew when I was there, whether by way of seeing or hearing me sing to him. Either way, this calmed him down and enabled him to peacefully fall asleep.

I often stayed with him for a while in his room, enjoying the feeling of being the father of this tiny baby who was my son. This time was precious to me and inspired me to feel tremendous appreciation for all that G-d had given me.

Other times, though, I was not able to remain in my child's room for any length of time. Either it was the middle of the night (when, out of sheer exhaustion, I would count the moments until I could go back to bed) or I simply had other things to do. Either way, I tried to slip out of the room before he went to sleep.

His reaction? Crying bitter tears.

So I devised a strategy. After singing him a song, I would whisper "shhh" while tiptoeing out of the room. This way, he would still hear my voice, even as the door slowly opened and closed, with me making my way to the other side of the door, outside his room.

Still waiting at the door, I would continue to whisper *sh-h-h* or sing another song, trying to impress upon my son that I was there for him, listening for him and taking care of him, even though he couldn't see me.

It didn't always work. He still wanted to be held by me or at least see me. Hearing me was not enough. But sometimes it sufficed, and that fascinated me.

I had a lot of time to reflect on these episodes, especially as my family grew and I found myself very often spending sleepless nights trying to put my kids to sleep. I came to realize that I am just like my little baby. When I can sense that my loving Father is near me (either because I "see" Him, "feel" I am being held by Him, or "hear" Him "talking" to me), I feel a strong sense of security, serenity, and inner peace. I am able to relax.

But if I feel that He has "left the room" and I am all alone "in the dark," I become afraid. I cry. I yearn for His closeness, for His warmth. And then I calm down again when He lifts me up.

Yet I realize that He, too, exercises my parenting strategy. By way of national historic miracles (such as the Exodus from Egypt) and daily wonders, He continues to demonstrate that He has given birth to us, sustained us early on, and will always be there for us. He then slips out of the room, whispering to us and watching over us. He wants us to feel independent, to be able to grow in this world. We don't necessarily "see" Him, though, which can make us feel somewhat lonely and lost.

I am often reminded of this parallel when I put my children to sleep. And I frequently use these quiet moments to marvel about how similar my relationship with my children is to my relationship with my Father in Heaven. Just as I love my children and would do anything for them, so too, our Father loves us and would do anything for our good. Just as my children are always on my mind and I would be at their sides in an instant (should that be necessary), so too, our Father is there for us, even when we may not feel that He is nearby.

Let us open up our eyes, ears, and hearts so that we may feel that deep, innate connection we have with Him. Let us feel secure in the knowledge that He is at the door — waiting, listening, caring — no matter how dark and lonely we feel inside the room.

> Let us open up our eyes, ears, and hearts so that we may feel that deep, innate connection we have with Him.

EMUNAH PESHUTAH

There is another facet of my spiritual growth that has developed since becoming a father — *emunah peshutah* (simple faith).

Simply put, I recognize that there is not only so much that is beyond our control, but there is also so little that we actually understand. As much as I may have understood that concept before having children, the following story demonstrates what I mean.

> *During the spring of 2012, I experienced one of the most frightening incidents of my fatherhood career to date. At the time, I was studying for my MBA. It was a typical Tuesday inasmuch as I was able to go home to be with my family for lunch because my classes for the day finished at eleven-thirty in the morning. But it was atypical the way I was greeted at the door — my son was screaming in a way I had never heard and my wife appeared quite shaken. After some deep breaths, my wife informed me that just a few moments prior to me*

walking in the door, she tripped down the stairs with our infant son and landed hard on the floor. She heard his head hit the tiles, but she wasn't sure of the extent of his injury. Was he injured or just very startled?

After ensuring that my wife was okay, I lovingly held my son, eventually calming him down. But he was simply not himself. He seemed more subdued than usual and it looked as though he was in pain, though the source of his pain was not clear to us. After all, he was only nine months old and was therefore unable to effectively communicate with us.

The doctor's office advised us that if he still wasn't back to his regular self in another couple of hours, we should bring him for an appointment with the doctor. And so we did. Immediately, the doctor checked for a head injury, but found nothing. He began to check other parts of our son's body to see where an injury might have occurred. Fascinatingly, when he stood my son up (while holding his hands), my son lifted his right foot, as if to show that he wasn't able to apply pressure there.

We were sent for further X-rays to ascertain the extent of the injury. While waiting for hours in the waiting room, we remember witnessing our son's gradual improvement. We almost decided to take him home because, in our estimation, everything was probably all right — and we were exhausted.

The ensuing X-rays, however, indicated otherwise. Yehoshua's femur bone had a crack right above his knee and they would have to put his entire leg, from his waist all the way down to his toes, in a cast for at least a month. Our precious little boy behaved so well while they plastered *his leg, after which they finally sent us on our way, with a referral to see a specialist the next morning at a different hospital to reinforce the cast with a layer of fiberglass.*

Through this dramatic episode, which felt like a rite of passage for new parents, my wife and I expressed how appreciative we were. Our nine-month-old's cracked femur bone — and all of the additional time and resources that would be required to help it heal efficiently — was not going to be easy for us, especially since we had a busy month coming up. Nevertheless, my wife and I felt a sense of gratitude. After all, we recognized that if he cracked his femur bone from a short fall (only a few steps up from the ground), it could have been much worse had he fallen from higher up the stairs.

But I remember being asked, somewhat incredulously: Appreciative?! What? He fell down the stairs! He cracked his femur bone! Dozens of hours were consumed going between doctors and hospitals, and his walking was delayed by a number of months! Appreciative?! Was I appreciative that G-d made my wife and baby fall?

And then an interesting parallel occurred to me. Passover was a few days away. Millions of Jews from around the globe were going to be celebrating this festival, celebrating the fact that G-d miraculously saved the Jews from 210 years of grueling slavery and led us into the Land of Israel.

But why celebrate? Why thank G-d for His wondrous miracles, such as the Ten Plagues and splitting the Red Sea? Didn't He put us in Egypt in the first place?! And

Didn't He put us in Egypt in the first place?! And if so, why should we thank Him for taking us out? Wasn't that His responsibility?

if so, why should we thank Him for taking us out? Wasn't that His responsibility?

This question weighed on me for a couple of days, until I watched a near-horrific incident which clarified everything.

> Over Passover, while my wife and I were taking a pleasant stroll down the street, we saw another young family about halfway up the block from where we were. The young mother was pushing her infant in a stroller, while the young father was walking alongside their toddler daughter. As if out of nowhere, the young girl turned and headed for the street, running at full speed. On cue, just like it happens in the movies, a car appeared, moving what seemed to be much faster than it should have on a side street. That's the moment when movies usually begin showing everything that happened in slow motion: the father's shocked expression as if he were thinking N-O-O-O-O as he chased after his daughter, while the mother watched helplessly, in horror, from the side.
>
> My wife and I stood there stunned, unsure how to prevent the seemingly inevitable from taking place. The girl was darting into the road and the fast-approaching car did not seem to see her.
>
> Then a miracle happened. The little girl tripped and fell hard onto the ground. Astounded, her mother and father scooped her up and embraced her, feeling renewed appreciation for having her in their lives.

After my wife and I let out a sigh of relief, we watched an interesting scenario unfold. The little girl was crying in pain and her parents were just so happy and appreciative. The girl looked at them, confused: *Don't you love me? Don't you care about me? Why are you so happy when I'm in so much pain?!*

What this little girl perceived as a terrible misfortune, the parents perceived as the greatest gift. Their prayers to save her at any cost were answered, but this little girl had no perception of the greater damage that could have occurred. For all I knew, she could have seen a toy on the other side of the street that she wanted. And now, not only did she not get the toy, but she fell and scraped her leg.

> *Don't you love me? Don't you care about me? Why are you so happy when I'm in so much pain?!*

This taught me a powerful message. Even though I consider myself an adult, I am very often like the little girl in the story. My scope of understanding is often limited, as there is a Higher Source whose view far surpasses that of my own. He sees what came before and what will come after; He knows what is truly best for me, even though I think I know better. And most importantly, He loves me and cares about me far more than I can possibly fathom.

> *And most importantly, He loves me and cares about me far more than I can possibly fathom.*

Just like the little girl in the story, I can cry and get upset that I didn't get the toy I wanted or that I got hurt. But if I recognize that what just happened was done with the greatest attention, love, and care possible, I rise above that arrogant spirit inside of me that feels like it knows it all.

My wife and son fell down the stairs. Thank you, G-d. Thank you. Understanding that for whatever reason there had to be a fall, I am so appreciative that it was only from the second step and not from the twelfth step; I am so appreciative that it was only a cracked femur bone and that my wife and son are otherwise all right; and I am so appreciative that You gave me the insight to view this incident with such an outlook.

That spirit is within all of us. We naturally feel like we know it all. We naturally like to feel that we are in charge. Letting go, though, is perhaps one of the greatest gifts we can give ourselves. Our leaning on the Source far wiser than ourselves provides us with the greatest sense of comfort, serenity, and happiness. As the cliché says, "Everything happens for a reason" — a reason that is ultimately for our greatest benefit. If we can internalize the fundamental principal that G-d loves each and every one of us far more than we can possibly comprehend, then we can begin to inch toward understanding how the different variables in our lives were uniquely tailored for us, allowing us to reach our individual mission in this world.

What you can accomplish, I cannot; and what I can accomplish, you cannot. Therefore, we each are given different circumstances in which we lead our lives. Our families, our unique talents, our geographical setting, and even the year in which we were born, are all designed solely with us in mind, serving as our guidepost for direction.

With this in mind, generation after generation, we have been celebrating Passover — thanking G-d for having taken us out slavery — because we understand that, notwithstanding the apparent need for us to be there (commentators provide numerous reasons for this), we are eternally appreciative for having been taken out in such a miraculous fashion.

The little girl who tripped taught me an invaluable lesson. As hard as her parents might have tried to explain to her that, had she not tripped she could have been hit by a car, she could not have understood. She was simply too young.

So, too, with us — at any age. If we can only recognize our smallness, or child-like characteristics, we can truly reach a level of greatness.

IN CONCLUSION

In conclusion, while dating, marriage, and parenting can be nerve-racking under the best of circumstances, for those of us who stutter (or face a different set of challenges), it can be exceptionally challenging. But it can also lead us to build an unprecedented relationship with our spouse and with G-d, encompassing beauty, depth, and previously unattainable trust.

Stuttering comes up, whether while dating, under the chuppah (marriage canopy), or while saying Kiddush (a prayer recited over wine on the Shabbat and festivals) in front of our spouses and children. And that is fine. If these things are approached with self-acceptance and confidence, they aren't just pitiful occurrences that others are willing to overlook, but rather something that will help us gain deeper levels of respect from everyone and help us in our roles as men and women, husbands and wives, and fathers and mothers.

8

BEING THE CHANGE

Be the change you want to see in the world.

— *Mahatma Gandhi*

WITH SWEATY PALMS, shaky legs, and parched lips, I was about to begin delivering a powerful speech to what was my largest audience yet. A Canadian synagogue had asked me to address their congregation at the most dramatic peak of the High Holidays (right before *Neilah*, the final prayer of Yom Kippur). The sanctuary was packed with men, women, and children — about one thousand people in all. Never before had I spoken before such a large audience.

"Be the change you want to see," I passionately proclaimed from the podium.

Quoting Mahatma Gandhi's famous line, I was encouraging the congregation to be the prime example of any positive transformation they wished to see around them, whether in their homes, community, or workplace. We too often project our internal deficiencies onto others, hoping for positive change only from those around us — because to truly look within, enough to stimulate real growth, we need to do some brutally honest introspection and self-evaluation.

At that moment, I was struck with an epiphany: *I was being the change that I wanted to see.* I was not just preaching about the attributes of resilience, self-acceptance, and positivity, but I was actually living it. I was doing what I loved to do and I was using my adversity (i.e., all the ways I had grown from my stutter) to help me do so. I was not just encouraging others to not allow their stutter (or other challenges) to hold them back in life, but I was leading by example in that regard. I was becoming the type of person that I wished to see in the world around me, and that infused me with a deep sense of genuine satisfaction.

> At that moment, I was struck with an epiphany: *I was being the change that I wanted to see.*

SUMMARY OF KEY CONCEPTS

The core messages of this book were very personal and part of my unique journey.

- My stutter was very difficult; it initially eroded my self-confidence and seriously called into question my relationship with G-d.

- After rebelling and ending up in Israel at the age of fifteen, I recognized that formulating the proper approach to my personal challenges was of critical importance, as this would directly impact my level of inner peace and true happiness.
- I was enthralled with the timeless advice of Rabbi Moshe Chaim Luzzatto (Ramchal), who encourages his readers to think about their purpose in this world. I realized, if I didn't know where I was going, how could I ever get there?
- I was surprised by the Ramchal's notion that I was brought into this world for true pleasure, because my life experiences were clearly not pointing in that direction.
- Yet I was inspired by the concept of ultimate reward taking place in the World to Come, with the level of pleasure corresponding to what I first earned in this world.
- This world was not intended to be relaxing like a spa, but rather like a gym, where my personal trainer (G-d), Who knows the full extent of my capabilities, will work me hard but never push me beyond that.
- Once I internalized that G-d loves me, cares about us all, and acts only in my best interest, I began to understand that my stutter — and all other variables in my life — were uniquely tailored for me, because they are exactly what I need to uniquely impact the world.
- Just like an actor being considered for an award, I too am judged by one sole criteria: how well I play the part into which I was placed.
- This newfound, refreshingly positive attitude gave me the strength to be confident about who I am — whether I'm in a social setting, a job interview, or in front of an audience.

- Because I have a tremendous amount to be grateful for, I should focus on appreciating all of the wonderful gifts in my life, be happy with who I am, and impact the world in the unique way that I can.

THE STUTTERING COMMUNITY

While writing this book, I familiarized myself with different factions within the stuttering community. And I must say that I have been truly inspired after meeting many leaders, speech therapists, and individuals who stutter; they embody the same attitude toward adversity that I am advocating in this book.

For instance, I was happy to learn that the Precision Fluency Shaping Program I attended when I was seventeen was renamed Fluency Plus — the "Plus" being the self-acceptance element. In addition, I was thrilled to learn about numerous virtual groups that offer guidance and support for those who stutter and those who are affected by it (i.e., parents of children who stutter), and I've even watched several inspiring TED Talks by people who stutter. There are also incredible conferences, documentaries, and blogs that echo a similar sentiment. It is a privilege to be a part of such a community.

My book, therefore, is intended to be a part of this growing trend of focusing on the person, not just the stutter; of focusing on self-acceptance, not just a cure; and of focusing on true happiness, not just survival. Most uniquely, though, my book addresses one stuttering-related issue that I

> My book, therefore, is intended to be a part of this growing trend of focusing on the person, not just the stutter; of focusing on self-acceptance, not just a cure; and of focusing on true happiness, not just survival.

have not seen anywhere else; it addresses spirituality. How do we deepen our connection to G-d through our stuttering? How do we embrace the challenge and truly recognize that it was given to us for our benefit?

There were questions I struggled with, questions that I know others have struggled with, and I therefore hope that the insights from my book shed some light on those important questions.

"REGULAR" ROLE MODELS

There are many ordinary people leading extraordinary lives. With specific regard to stuttering, though, I would like to highlight two people whose stories truly moved me. Even though there are many "famous" people who stutter (see appendix 3), I have found it helpful to learn from "ordinary," more relatable people.

Parker Mantell

Originally from Memphis, Tennessee, twenty-one-year-old Parker Mantell delivered Indiana University's 2014 commencement address, which subsequently went viral on YouTube. The noteworthy part of it is that when Parker ascended the podium to begin his address, he immediately confessed to the seventeen thousand-strong audience that he might not have not been the most obvious candidate for this speech.

> *As a person who stutters, I can be no more certain that in this room and in this hall are thousands of people who are far more talented at public speaking than I am. At the same time, however, I can be no more certain that the message I have to share is one that must be heard.*

Mentioning Beethoven's deafness, Ray Charles' blindness, and Albert Einstein's dyslexia, all of which were "disabilities" that failed to get in the way of their success, he urged his classmates to rise above any doubts they may have regarding their true abilities. "Imagine what you are depriving our world of if you never dare to achieve your purpose."

In his epic speech, in which he noticeably stuttered, he credited Indiana University with instilling in him the confidence to pursue his dreams, rather than keeping them at bay because of his speech impediment. The university encouraged him to go after numerous high-profile internships that found him answering thousands of calls for House Majority Leader Eric Cantor, conducting tours of the Capitol for Florida Senator Marco Rubio, and making outreach calls for New Jersey Governor Chris Christie.

He urged his classmates to rise above any doubts they may have regarding their true abilities. "Imagine what you are depriving our world of if you never dare to achieve your purpose."

> *I mention those experiences not out of individual pride or out of vanity, but rather out of the desire to share Indiana University's role in dispelling the idea that someone who is barely able to talk for himself can dream big enough to talk for public servants. While any other university might have instructed me to manage those expectations, IU taught me to grow through them.*

He then urged his classmates to reach for their dreams, regardless of the challenges that lie before them, and concluded with the following:

Being the Change

Today, I issue the Indiana University challenge to you.

I challenge you to stop believing in those who cast doubt upon you and to start believing in yourselves.

I challenge you to shift your thinking such that when opportunities come before you, you don't ask yourself, Why me — you ask yourself, Why not me!

I challenge you, therefore, to take a step forward — to dare to do what others have doubted that you can.

I challenge you to take that step forward not despite your disabilities, your hurdles, or your hesitancies, but because of them.

I challenge you to take that step forward not because doing so would be easy, but as President Kennedy once declared, because it would be hard.

Yet, above all, I challenge you to take that step forward because…as Indiana University has taught us, it is possible.

David

Uri Schneider, the co-director of Schneider Speech (with offices in New York and Israel), meets many different kinds of clients from all over the world. Therefore, it was hardly surprising when AMBI, Israel's nonprofit organization helping those who stutter, connected him with a young man named David[21], who was from a small town in Northern Israel.

Early in their first session, Uri quickly discovered why David had showed up. He was about to enter the army and he hoped to enlist

---

21   Name changed for anonymity purposes.

in *Shaldag*, an elite unit within the Israeli Defense Forces, whose mission is to deploy undetected into hostile environments to conduct special reconnaissance missions, just like his father and grandfather had done when they were younger. As a strong, ambitious young man with a dedicated work ethic, he wasn't nervous about any of the physical tryouts; rather, he was worried only about one small part of the grueling interview process. Following a week of sleep deprivation and workouts that completely wear down the applicants, there is a face-to-face interview with five psychologists to determine whether they can handle the intensity of the unit. For David, that session seemed to have stuttering written all over it, so he came to Uri to ask what to do.

David had already been through a number of tests, rising to the top out of hundreds of fit candidates. The only potential issue for him was his stutter. He had been very conservative his whole life, both academically and socially, finding ways to circumvent speaking situations. But here it was inevitable.

How should he best prepare for this interview? Should he focus on stuttering for the two months leading up to the interview or push off the entrance exam for another eight months to try to completely eradicate any remnant of the impediment?

After consulting with others, Uri suggested that he take it head-on. There was no reason to push it off, and the probability was that if he had been stuttering this long, he would probably stutter in the interview, even if it was eight months later.

So with the big day approaching, Uri advised him as follows:

> With all the strategies and the work you have done, in that situation — exhausted and worn out, deliberately so

by the program — there is no question that you will stutter when sitting in front of those five highly skilled and trained professionals who will be interviewing and evaluating you. Therefore, I think that the best defense is a solid offense. Going into the interview, be open about your stutter. Tell them, "I stutter. It is not an emotional problem; it is not a cognitive problem. I can be a great soldier."

David was visibly hesitant; after all, he had spent his adolescence hiding from his stutter, embarrassed by its implications. And now, when he was at the cusp of attaining his lifelong goal, he would have to bring it up front and center?

Uri was understanding, yet persistent. "Talk it over with your parents," he suggested. "See what they have to say about this plan."

Everyone felt it was a good plan.

Several weeks later, the fated phone call came in.

"Uri, I got in." Then, through tears, David continued, "It went really well. When I went in, the first thing I told them, through my broken speech, was as follows: "This thing that I do, I have been doing it since I was a kid. I have done well in school, in national youth movements, leadership roles, and more. It is neither a cognitive problem nor an emotional problem. It also cannot stop me from being an excellent soldier. What do you want to ask me?"

"That's amazing!" Uri exclaimed.

"There's even more." David enthusiastically continued, "After I was

He explained that the moment I entered the room and confidently prefaced the discussion with the fact that I stuttered (while stuttering!), they knew that I had it inside of me to be in the Special Forces.

accepted, I bumped into one of the psychologists. And do you know what he told me? He explained that the moment I entered the room and confidently prefaced the discussion with the fact that I stuttered (while stuttering!), they knew that I had it inside of me to be in the Special Forces."

David eventually dropped out of *Shaldag* to join *Duvdevan*, a different elite unit in the Israeli army, where he felt he would be happier. There, he requested to become an officer, but was turned down. "You're a good soldier. But with your speech, how would you lead other soldiers? You're not what we're looking for."

Persistent and confident, David ultimately convinced his supervisors to allow him to become an officer. And in the summer of 2014, David — along with his stutter — led a group of soldiers into battle, in Operation Protective Edge.

TRUE HEROES

Parker and David are regular people, yet true heroes. They are two examples of people who are "being the change." (I have been privileged to meet many more since I began writing this book.) They decided to embrace their challenge of stuttering and confidently lead their lives, thereby making their own positive impact on the world around them.

Parker and David are regular people, yet true heroes.

Let us follow their lead; let us all "be the change."

CONCLUSION

Happiness is a journey, not a destination.

— *Alfred D. Souza*

AFTER RELOCATING WITH my family to Israel and finishing my MBA at Tel Aviv University, I became active in the high tech start-up scene, working in business development roles at early stage start-ups and serving as a mentor at a Jerusalem-based entrepreneurship accelerator. I have learned much about business, entrepreneurship, and life lessons along the way, but what strikes me the most is the similarity between successful entrepreneurs and the concepts I previously explained in this book.

Some of the most important things that an entrepreneur must do in order to succeed are to define a clear vision for the company, be passionate about the product/service, and confidently overcome obstacles along the way.

Previously, I have described the important ingredients for my personal success:

Vision: What is my purpose? Where am I headed? What is my mission?

Passion: Do I appreciate myself? Am I living with zest, with enthusiasm?

Adversity: Do I accept my unique challenges? Am I growing through them?

START-UP ENTREPRENEURS

I would like to point out two entrepreneurs that engendered these characteristics and built hugely successful companies as a result.

The first example is the late Steve Jobs, co-founder and former CEO of Apple. In 1985, Jobs was pushed out of Apple, the company he started. But he took it as a blessing in disguise. After being rejected to fly on the Space Shuttle Challenger as a civilian astronaut, he decided to try something new — he purchased an animation studio, which would later be known as Pixar. Eventually, when he was asked to rejoin Apple as CEO in 1997 to revitalize the company, he credits his ensuing success to the creativity and know-how he gleaned during his time at Pixar, an invaluable experience which would have never happened had he not been booted from Apple in the first place.

Jobs's vision for Apple, passion for the product, and growth through his adversity helped build Apple into one of the most successful companies of our times.

Another example that wonderfully illustrates this concept is the case of Jan Koum, from WhatsApp. After finishing a stint with Yahoo, Koum applied for a job at Facebook — but was rejected. So, he decided to launch a small start-up of his own, one that would provide users with a simple, intuitive approach to private and group messaging.

However, the early version of WhatsApp kept crashing and Koum was about to leave the fledgling, bootstrapped startup to get a real job.

But his friend and co-founder, Brian Acton, convinced him to stay and give it one more shot. He agreed, and as a result was even more determined to build a foolproof product.[22]

Then, just four-and-a-half years after being rejected for a job at Facebook, Koum sold his startup back to Mark Zuckerberg and his Facebook team for a staggering $22 billion!

Then, just four-and-a-half years after being rejected for a job at Facebook, Koum sold his startup back to Mark Zuckerberg and his Facebook team for a staggering $22 billion!

PARALLEL TO ADVERSITY

I try to imagine what it must have been like to be Jobs or Koum in **the early** days of Apple or WhatsApp. They exuded a passion for their **product** and a strong vision for the future. They were also not going to let minor setbacks — such as being ousted by their company or technology glitches — prevent them from achieving their dream.

As such, they must have felt a deep sense of mission — not just when their companies became known as two of the most successful technology startups in history, but also throughout the entire process of building them up, viewing their setbacks as vehicles for success.

The same principle applies to dealing with adversity.

If we only recognize that we have been endowed with a unique mission and that our adversity is lovingly meted out to guide us along

---

22 As of April 2015, WhatsApp had eight hundred million active users worldwide. Clearly, WhatsApp became a great success.

that track, we would be infused with passion for our daily lives and the strength to overcome whatever is sent our way.

If we only recognized that by growing through our challenges we are accruing incomprehensible reward, we would feel much more meaning, purpose, and true happiness throughout the entire process.

Jobs and Koum understood that even though it was very difficult to design, build, and grow their products, it still gave them an enormous sense of satisfaction to know that they were on the right path to positively impacting the world and becoming hugely successful.

A JOURNEY, NOT A DESTINATION

This reminds me of one of my favorite quotes, "Happiness is a journey, not a destination."

Two different kinds of people can be on the same journey, be it career-oriented, geographical, or spiritual. One is constantly stressed, talking obsessively about "getting there," and the other is peacefully enjoying the ride itself, while also enthusiastic about what lies ahead. (Many of us have met both kinds of people.)

As a result, one of them is happy throughout, while the other delays his feeling of satisfaction until the end — a destination that is often elusive.

We are all on a journey through life. Why not enjoy it? This is truly the message that has helped me, more and more, since my teenage years.

> *We are all on a journey through life. Why not enjoy it?*

When my severe stutter (and other challenges) seemed totally random, it was just too painful to bear. There was no meaning behind

Conclusion 175

them. I felt lost and all alone. My pain was exacerbated by the apparent meaninglessness, which made it exceptionally difficult to cope. As Rebbetzin Esther Jungreis writes in her inspiring book *Life is a Test*, "S minus M equals D (Suffering – Meaning = Depression)."

Similarly, Austrian neurologist, psychiatrist, and Holocaust survivor, Viktor Frankl, quotes in his book, *The Unheard Cry for Meaning*, a study of sixty students at American universities who had attempted suicide. Eighty-five percent of those students explained that the reason they tried to kill themselves was because "life seemed meaningless." Frankl concludes, therefore, that man's search for meaning should be of prime importance.

As such, once I was able to incorporate more meaning into my life, by delving into the true purpose behind the world and, more importantly, my unique life, things seemed to come together to form a beautiful tapestry, even though the full picture is beyond my comprehension.

At this stage in my life, when I reflect back on my different experiences, I begin to see the handiwork of G-d's artistic, magnificent work. More and more, when I look back on my years of pain, frustration, and anger (regarding my stutter), I catch a glimpse of G-d's masterful plan in helping me become the person I am today.

Empowered by this knowledge, I am determined to feel happy while on my continued journey through life (regardless of what comes my way), not just at the end, when I reflect back and recognize that everything served a purpose.

TWO CONCLUDING STORIES

I would like to end with two more inspiring stories and concluding thoughts.

Story #1

Years ago, I heard the following memorable story from Rabbi Tuvia Lieff, a popular congregational rabbi from Brooklyn, New York. He was describing a young woman in his community who seemed rather typical (nice character traits, etc.), but had an unusual obsession with roller coasters. He went on to say that this woman was actually not typical at all — in fact, she was blind.

When asked by her father why she loved the biggest, scariest, and loopiest roller coasters, she explained as follows:

> *Living life as a blind woman is not easy. There are twists and turns, and it can be quite uncomfortable. That's why I love roller coasters. No matter how big or frightening the ride can be, I am reminded that I am safely riding on a custom-built track and will be all right. G-d runs the show; He made me blind. Regardless of how difficult my life can get, I am comforted in knowing that there is meaning, purpose, and direction behind my blindness.*

Incredible.

Story #2

I heard the following story from Rabbi Dr. Abraham J. Twerski, a noted psychiatrist and author of more than sixty books, at a lecture he gave in Toronto.

With some extra time on his hands while strolling around Manhattan, Rabbi Twerski decided to attend an Alcoholics Anonymous meeting

Conclusion 177

near Times Square. Specializing in substance abuse, he always found these meetings especially insightful. Inside, each participant began to describe his/her path to sobriety. The seemingly typical meeting was then greatly enhanced by the last participant's remarks. After stating her name and length of time she had been sober, she shared with the group the following story:

> I am a huge football fan. I haven't missed a game all season. I'm the kind of fan who yells at the television throughout the game. A little while ago, I had to travel for work and my flight was scheduled for game time. Regrettably, there was nothing I could do about it but to ask my roommate to tape the game for me, so I could watch it from beginning to end when I returned. I stressed, though, that she should NOT tell me who won.
>
> Upon returning from my short trip, my roommate handed me the tape, and with a grin on her face, she said, "We won." I was furious! She just spoiled the entire game for me!
>
> But like any die-hard fan, I watched the game anyway. Toward the end of the third quarter, the Jets were down. This is when, under other circumstances, I would have been yelling at the coach for every decision he made. Surprisingly, though, I found myself watching the game with a sense of serenity I never before felt at such a pivotal point. Because I knew that we were ultimately going to win, it didn't really upset me that we were losing, regardless of how dire the circumstances seemed to be.

Because I knew that we were ultimately going to win, it didn't really upset me that we were losing

178 THE GIFT OF STUTTERING

This was a revelation for me. As a recovering alcoholic, I have been through very challenging patches, during which it seemed like I would never be able to succeed. Sometimes it is simply too hard to resist the urge to take another drink.

But then I remind myself of the game that I watched. I, too, know that I will "win"; G-d is on my side and is helping me through. Therefore, even when it seems to be the end and all odds are stacked against me, I am reassured by the knowledge that He is on my side, helping me through. I, too, will ultimately win.

FINAL THOUGHTS

I am both humbled and appreciative that I am living my dream.

It is not because I stopped stuttering, because I still do. And it is not because life is easy, because it is not. Rather, it is because I feel a sense of purpose and satisfaction from what I am doing and where I am going. I have come to recognize that my circumstances are perfectly designed for me, and I am therefore infused with recognition that I am living with a unique sense of purpose and mission, leading to true happiness.

Life is beautiful.

My friend Gil recently pointed out to me that G-d gave each person a unique set of fingerprints, hinting to us that we can each "touch" the world in a distinct way. No two people are alike, nor are their missions identical. We can each accomplish different things, and G-d gave us the perfect set of skills and resources to do so.

In my teenage years, I used to complain that "life is complicated." I remember one of my rabbis responding with genuine sincerity, "Life is actually pretty simple."

It took me years to understand what he meant, and he is right. We don't understand it all. But when we recognize that we aren't fully capable of understanding it all (and leave that job up to the loving Creator of the world), it should leave us with a true sense of serenity.

I still stutter. And I am fine with it. There are times when it comes up more often, and sometimes less often. But regardless of its frequency and severity, I always try to remind myself of the timeless messages I have tried to convey in this book.

I am also proud to say that my stutter has not been holding me back. In business, I mentor entrepreneurs on how to strategically build their start-ups and I often deliver presentations at my office. Over the last ten years, I have delivered hundreds of lectures around the world, including leadership programs in Europe and Australia, a Daf Yomi *shiur* (daily Talmud class) to young professionals in a Tel Aviv suburb, and weekly classes to university students at Bar Ilan University.

Astounding? Perhaps. But not because my stutter magically disappeared, but rather because I have become comfortable with it — both in concept and in practice.

In fact, my stutter still comes up. Often. For instance, one of those words which I still often get stuck on is *kideshanu* (a Hebrew word in many blessings). Not only does it come up weekly during Kiddush (a prayer said aloud on Friday night) when I say the blessing aloud, but it also comes up during *Birchat Kohanim* (Priestly Blessing recited during prayers), which is recited daily in Israel.

Hearing me consistently pause before the same word, numerous people have asked me what I'm thinking before saying that word. As I am being sheltered by my prayer shawl, they can't see that I am merely struggling to get the word out.

I know that I have truly grown when I can respond with a chuckle, "I wish I was so holy, but I just have a stutter."

I still have a long way to go, as we all do. So let us get out there. Let us live. Whether we are challenged with a stutter or any other form of adversity, let us recognize that it is given with the utmost love — and it is given to help us reach our full potential.

Let's live life. Let's love life. Let's recognize and appreciate G-d's gifts, however they may be packaged. And leveraging *all* the resources that we have been given, challenges included, let us each make our own unique mark on the world.

APPENDIX 1

SUCCINCT STUTTERING-RELATED ADVICE

FOR THOSE OF YOU WITH A STUTTER

Review the valuable advice from George Springer, twenty-five-year-old outfielder with the Houston Astros (a major league baseball team):

> I was that kid who didn't want to speak in class and tried to avoid certain situations. But then, once I just accepted it [stuttering], it actually changed my outlook on pretty much everything and made me a lot happier with myself...Embrace it and don't let it prevent you from doing the things that you want to do in life.

It's rough, I know. But accept it, embrace it. Be happy with who you are. Appreciate the life you lead, *all* the gifts G-d has given you and move forward. Connect with a reliable speech therapist who sees you as a person with emotions, abilities, and extraordinary potential. Rather than expecting the stutter to disappear, pray for the strength to deal with it positively.

Introduce yourself to those you otherwise wouldn't have. Do not hesitate to speak in public, for the audience can gain tremendous value from what you have to say — and how you say it.

And make sure to hold your head up high: G-d gives his hardest battles to His strongest soldiers.

FOR PARENTS OF CHILDREN WHO STUTTER

The closing ceremonies of the National Stuttering Association's annual conference (July 2015 in Baltimore, MD) included a speech by a woman who attended the conference for the first time, at the behest of her thirty-three-year-old son who stuttered. She relayed a powerful story about breaking down in tears at a parents' workshop where she had to "practice" stuttering, because it made her realize that she could barely function — even for just a few minutes — doing what her son has been doing all day, every day, for thirty years. She closed by telling all the parents in the room that they had raised some of the strongest people in the world.

It is painful to watch your child struggle. I know; I watched my parents go through it. Know that this is a challenge for you too. For your child's sake, though, I respectfully request that you have patience, engender warmth and love, and express unconditional acceptance. I have heard gut-wrenching stories of children and teenagers who are afraid to speak in their own homes. And while I am confident that their parents have loving intentions (i.e., to "fix" their child's stutter), it's critical to recognize that the greatest way to help your child is to provide a safe zone, where he/she can feel comfortable speaking without inhibition.

Finally, I would like to quote my mother's poignant advice, as featured in an article she wrote for Aish.com, titled "Tongue Untied":

> As a parent of a stutterer, I offer the following suggestions to those in the same position:
>
> Encourage your child to talk. Let him know that it is what he says — not how he says it — that is important.
>
> Enlist the help of a speech therapist. If the first professional you try isn't a good match, find another when the person is ready and willing to work at it. The methods will help. They will not cure him, per se, but practicing will help him gain the confidence to express himself.
>
> Meet with the speech therapist to find out how you, his parents and his teachers, can further help him.
>
> Pray. Pray that the speech impediment does not hinder your child, but that it serves to propel him to even greater heights and accomplishments.
>
> We would not tell a person with crooked teeth not to smile; we would not tell a person who limps to limit his walking in public. Encourage your child to talk. Let him know there is value to everything he has to say, no matter how difficult it may be for him to get the words out.

FOR EVERYONE WHO COMES INTO CONTACT WITH THOSE WHO STUTTER

In an article titled, "What Not to Do When in a Conversation with Someone Who Stutters," Madeline Wahl, Associate Editor of Blogs & Community at *The Huffington Post*, succinctly described her stuttering-related experience as follows:

> *I've seen every physical manifestation of irritation appear in front of me — from people rolling their eyes and tapping their feet, to crossing their arms and looking off in the distance, to exhaling loudly, or just starting a new conversation right over what I was trying to say.*

Please don't do that to us. Be kind to those of us who stutter. Please don't finish our sentences, because even though you don't intend to do so, you are thereby making us feel inadequate. While we stutter, please maintain eye contact with us and please don't check your phone or watch — it makes us feel rushed. Also, please don't pretend to be our speech therapist by asking us take a deep breath and try again. As if we didn't know that.

I know you only want to help; so please help by creating a warm, accepting environment in which we can stutter without feeling anxious about what you will now think about us. Wait patiently for us to finish our thoughts. It's worth it; we have valuable insights to share.

Please don't treat us any differently; we are just like you, even though we exhibit different speech patterns. We all have our differences.

Appreciate your ability to speak fluently. It doesn't make you any better than us, but it does impose upon you the added responsibility to express your appreciation for it, and to treat those of us who stutter with sensitivity, dignity, and respect.

APPENDIX 2

STUTTERING-RELATED RESOURCES

In our generation, we are blessed with a plethora of stuttering-related resources, including organizations, documentaries, and support groups. As such, please note that the following is only a partial list of what currently exists.[23] For more information and/or for specific questions, please do not hesitate to contact me directly. I would be happy to try to connect you with resources that are most relevant to your personalized needs.

American Board of Fluency and Fluency Disorders (ABFFD) — Stuttering specialists are speech-language pathologists who have been recognized by the ABFFD as having achieved advanced training and clinical skill for working with people who stutter and their families. A list of Board-Certified Specialists in Fluency Disorders (BCS-F) can be found at stutteringspecialists.org.

---

23 Loosely taken from the National Stuttering Foundation's website.

American Institute for Stuttering (AIS) — Located in New York City, the American Institute for Stuttering is a leading non-profit organization in the United States that offers state-of-the-art treatment to people who stutter, and support to their families. AIS also provides clinical training to speech-language pathologists (SLP) interested in acquiring special expertise in stuttering treatment. See stutteringtreatment.org for more information.

American Speech-Language-Hearing Association (ASHA) — ASHA is the professional association for speech-language pathologists. ASHA's Special Interest Division for Fluency and Fluency Disorders (DIV-4) consists of clinicians and researchers who have expressed a particular interest in stuttering. See asha.org for more information.

British Stammering Association (BSA) — BSA is the only national organization in the United Kingdom for adults and children who stammer, and is run by people who stammer. See stammering.org for more information.

Friends — A national organization created to provide a network of love and support for children and teenagers who stutter, their families, and the professionals who work with them. See friendswhostutter.org for more information.

International Stuttering Association — The International Stuttering Association is made up of national groups that are guided by a board of directors, with the aim of helping others understand stuttering. See isastutter.org for more information.

Israel Stuttering Association — A charity since 1999, AMBI is an Israeli-based non-profit organization that supports people who stutter and their families. The name, AMBI, is an acronym made up from the initial letters of the Association's official Hebrew name. See ambi.org.il for more information.

National Stuttering Association (NSA) — The NSA is a non-profit organization dedicated to bringing hope and empowerment to children and adults who stutter, their families, and professionals, through support, education, advocacy, and research. They host a popular annual conference to empower those who are affected by stuttering. See westutter.org for more information.

Say — Say's mission is to empower young people who stutter and inspire the world to treat them with compassion and respect so they can achieve their dreams. Their vision is a world where every voice matters. See say.org for more information.

Speech & Stuttering Institute — The Speech & Stuttering Institute is based in Toronto, Canada and its mandate is three-fold: to provide clinical service, to educate and train professionals throughout the province, and to engage in cutting-edge research to unearth the root causes of speech-related challenges in order to find the most effective treatment methods. See speechandstuttering.com for more information.

Stuttering Foundation of America (SFA) — SFA provides free online resources, services, and support to those who stutter and their families, as well as support for research into the causes of stuttering. See stutteringhelp.org for more information.

StutterTalk — A weekly podcast where the host talks openly about stuttering, and interviews people who stutter and leaders in the field. See stuttertalk.com for more information.

APPENDIX 3

SOME NOTABLE PEOPLE WHO STUTTER(ED)

Just saying...we are in good company. And we have no excuse for not being as great as we can be! This list has been loosely taken from the National Stuttering Foundation's website.

Taro Alexander — Actor, teacher, and founder of Our Time and Our Time Theatre Company

Dennis Barsema — Silicon Valley executive

Clara Barton — Pioneering nurse during the American Civil War who founded the American Red Cross

Rabbi Ari Bensoussan — Popular teacher, mentor, and motivational speaker

P.F. Bentley — Award-winning photographer known for his photos of presidents

Joseph Biden — Former US senator and current vice president of the United States

Arthur M. Blank — Co-founder of Home Depot and owner of the NFL's Atlanta Falcons

Jeffrey Blitz — Award-winning film director, producer, and screenwriter

Emily Blunt — Award-winning English-born actress

Robert Boyle — Anglo-Irish natural philosopher, chemist, physicist, and inventor born in Ireland

Ernie Canadeo — Founder and CEO of a successful advertising agency, and past chairman of the National Stuttering Association

Sir Winston Churchill — Prime minister of the United Kingdom, 1940 – 1945 and 1951 – 1955

Johnny Damon — All-star and two-time World Series champion outfielder for the New York Yankees

Charles Darwin — English naturalist and geologist, best known for his contributions to evolutionary theory

Demosthenes — Prominent Greek statesman and orator of ancient Athens

Sander Flaum — CEO of Flaum Partners, a consulting firm serving the pharmaceutical and biotech industries

Annie Glenn — Inductee into the National Stuttering Association Hall of Fame and wife of astronaut and senator John Glenn

The Guangxu Emperor — The eleventh emperor of the Qing Dynasty and the ninth Qing emperor to rule over China

Some Notable People Who Stutter(ed)

Sophie Gustafson — Swedish golfer who won twenty-eight titles on the most prestigious tours and earned over $6.3 million

Ron Harper — Retired NBA basketball player

Russ Hicks — Award-winning public speaker in Toastmasters

Neal Jeffrey — Associate pastor of a mega-church in Dallas; former professional football player

Marty Jezer — Writer and political activist

James Earl Jones — Award-winning actor

B.B. King — American blues singer, songwriter, and guitarist

Nana Kinomi — Japanese actress and singer

Scatman John Larkin — Jazz musician and poet

Nobby Lewandowski — Successful businessman and motivational speaker, also former professional baseball player

Bob Love — Legendary basketball star

Gerald A. Maguire, MD — Professor and chair of psychiatry and neuroscience at UC Riverside School of Medicine, distinguished fellow of the APA

Walt Manning — Speech-language pathologist, professor at the University of Memphis, and author of textbooks on stuttering

Kenyon Martin — First overall draft pick in the 2000 NBA draft; NBA all-star in 2003 – 2004; member of Team USA

John Melendez — Television personality and writer

Larry Molt — Speech-language pathologist and director of the neuroprocesses laboratory at Auburn University

Marilyn Monroe — Hollywood personality, famous for her whispering tone of voice (used to cover up her stutter)

Moses — Most important teacher in all of history

Sir Isaac Newton — English physicist and mathematician who is widely recognized as one of the most influential scientists of all time

Jack Paar — Radio and television comedian

Adrian Peterson — NFL running back

Byron Pitts — Reporter for "CBS News"

Bob Quesal — Speech-language pathologist, professor at Western Illinois University, and prominent researcher on stuttering

Alan Rabinowitz — Zoologist and conservationist known for his work in protecting endangered species

Lee Reeves — Founded one of the first local stuttering support groups

Peter Reitzes — Speech-language pathologist; co-founder of the StutterTalk podcast

John Stossel — Emmy-award winner and former co-anchor for the ABC news show "20/20"

Mel Tillis — Legendary country singer and songwriter

Jack Welch — Retired CEO of General Electric and authority on business leadership

Bruce Willis — Actor, producer, and singer

Tiger Woods — One of the most successful golfers of all time

APPENDIX 4

DID MOSHE RABBEINU STUTTER?

BASED ON ESSAYS BY RABBI MENACHEM POSNER AND ALEX MAGED

"DID YOU KNOW that Moshe Rabbeinu stuttered too?" I am constantly asked. People want to comfort me by showing that I am in good company. And it actually helps. Being that my name is Moshe and I stutter, I feel a special connection with the most famous and important teacher in all of Jewish history — Moshe Rabbeinu.

Let's first gain a deeper understanding on how the classic commentaries describe Moshe's speech impediment and then we can glean invaluable lessons from this remarkable story.

The entire discussion stems from a conversation that G-d had with Moshe, trying to convince him to redeem the Jewish People who were enslaved in Egypt. Initially resisting being God's messenger because of his speech, Moshe pleads, "Please, G-d, I have never been a man of words...I am heavy of mouth and heavy of tongue,"[24] and therefore unsuitable for the leadership role.

There is a well-known Midrash behind this, whereby Moshe injured himself as a small child when he put a burning coal in his mouth.[25] Yet on what basis did popular opinion conclude that burning one's tongue on coals would result in a stutter?

It must have been the succinct assertion of eleventh-century rabbinical scholar, Rabbi Shlomo Yitzchaki (commonly known as Rashi), the most widely used Biblical commentary. Occasionally, to better explain a word or phrase, Rashi translates Biblical Hebrew words into medieval French. In this case, he used the medieval French noun *balbus*,[26] "stuttering or stammering" (from which comes the modern French verb *balbutier*, "to stutter"), to which later glossarists added the Old German *stammeler*, "a stutterer."

Writing several decades after Rashi, Avraham Ibn Ezra expanded upon this idea, stating that Moshe "found it very challenging to vocalize certain letters." And Rabbi Yaakov Tzvi Mecklenburg, nineteenth-century German rabbi and scholar, takes it a step further by actually listing one set of phonemes that Moshe struggled to pronounce due to his "heavy tongue," and a second set which Moshe struggled to pronounce due to his "heavy mouth."

Rashi's grandson, Rabbi Shmuel Ben Meir (known by his acronym, Rashbam), rejects this line of reasoning. He argues that Moshe's problem had nothing to do with stuttering (or any other speech impediment

---

24   *Shemot* 4:10.
25   *Shemot Rabbah* 1:26.
26   *Shemot* 4:10.

for that matter); rather, he was simply ill-equipped to speak Egyptian because he had fled from there in his youth. Thirteenth-century French rabbi, Chezkia ben Manoach (otherwise known as Chizkuni) agrees with Rashbam: "Moshe had forgotten the Egyptian language."

Others commentators — such as Ramban (twelfth century), Alshich (sixteenth century), and Malbim (nineteenth century) — fundamentally agree with Rashi that Moshe had a speech impediment, but they don't attempt to discern which type. Instead, they focus on Moshe's concern about it: Perplexed by his inability to speak fluently, Moshe is questioning whether G-d will enable him to adequately express himself to both the Egyptians' pharoah and the Jewish People, in his quest to redeem them from slavery. For if not, how could he possibly succeed in his mission?

Finally, the sixteenth-century Rabbi Yehuda Loew (well known as the Maharal of Prague) teaches a novel, kabbalistic approach. "Moshe was far removed from the material world. Therefore, he did not possess the power of speech, for it is a distinctly physical characteristic."[27]

While the mystical mechanics of Maharal's theory are far too complex for this appendix, Rabbi Akiva Tatz (contemporary Jewish scholar from London) provides a useful summary in his popular book, *The Thinking Jewish Teenager's Guide to Life*.

> Moshe was living in a world of truth [and as such, he] knew the essence of things as they really are, far beyond the level of the words which attempt to describe them. Things grasped thus prophetically, essentially, could never be shrunk into words.

---

27   *Gevurot Hashem*, chap. 28.

Dr. Erica Brown, not referring directly to the Maharal, puts it even more simply in her book *Leadership in the Wilderness*, "Moshe...was unable to make small talk. He was preoccupied with heavy, weighty matters."

As we have seen, all of the classic commentaries agree that Moshe had some form of a speech impediment. Fourteenth-century Sage, Rabbi Nissim ben Reuben (known as Ran),[28] is bothered by this. He asks, Why, then, would G-d choose Moshe as his mouthpiece for the world's important teaching mission? Shouldn't He have chosen a more charismatic, well-spoken orator for the role?

He poignantly answers as follows: Had Moshe been an eloquent and gifted speaker, there would always be room for skeptics to claim that the Jewish People accepted the Torah, its truths and its mandates, only as a result of Moshe's charisma. But because the Jewish People struggled to understand Moshe, it became eminently clear that they did not accept the Torah because they were captivated by Moshe, but rather because it was clearly the unadulterated word of G-d.

Samson Raphael Hirsch, a brilliant nineteenth-century German rabbi, echoes this sentiment.

> *Because you sense, through and through, that you lack even the slightest aptitude to venture upon — let alone accomplish — such a mission by your own human powers, precisely for this reason you are the one who is best suited to carry out My mission.*[29]

He then follows with a powerful one-liner (that I highlighted in my personal copy of his book many years ago), "Your very inadequacy will

---

28   *Derashot HaRan*, derush 3.
29   *The Hirsch Chumash, Shemot* 3:12.

attest to the divine character of your mission." There is a powerful lesson to be learned from this story. Moshe was hesitant — due to his speech impediment (that many assume to be a stutter) — to be dispatched on the colossally important mission of saving the Jewish People. But when G-d reassured him that He was the One who gave him the impediment and He was the one who was commanding him to assume this leadership post, Moshe acceded to the mission.

As such, his accepting the role was not contingent on G-d removing his stutter. He was going to roll with G-d's plan. He finally recognized that there was meaning and purpose behind his speech (even though he might not have fully understood it), which gave him the strength to accept his stutter and pursue his destiny as the most important orator in history.

We each have a unique, important mission, too. Let us learn from Moshe's example and not allow our impediments (be it stuttering or otherwise) to prevent us from accomplishing it!

APPENDIX 5

RECOMMENDED READING LIST

USING MY CHALLENGE with stuttering as the backdrop, this book touches upon one of the most fundamental and age-old theological questions, Why do bad things happen to good people? It is therefore important to remind you that this book is not intended to be a dissertation on the topic and cover the classic sources that grapple with this question; rather, it is a vehicle to convey my personal story, along with light, anecdotal insights I gleaned along the way.

Nevertheless, I highly recommend a more thorough investigation into this fascinating topic, as I am confident that the takeaways will further inspire readers to discover meaning and purpose behind personal struggles and national tragedies.

Below are some of the contemporary Jewish books (written in English) that directly address this topic:

Aiken, Lisa. *Why Me, God?: A Jewish Guide for Coping with Suffering.* Jason Aronson Inc, 1996.

Blech, Benjamin. *If God Is Good, Why Is the World So Bad?* Simcha Press, 2003.

Jungreis, Esther. *Life Is a Test.* Mesorah Publications, 2006.

Kirzner, Yitzchok. *Making Sense of Suffering: A Jewish Approach.* Mesorah Publications, 2002.

Mandell, Sherri. *The Blessing of a Broken Heart.* Maggid, 2000.

Moskoff, Yerachmiel. *This Too Is for the Best.* Mosaica Press, 2013.

APPENDIX 6

CROWDFUNDING CAMPAIGN — SUMMARY AND DEDICATIONS

THANKS TO THE generosity of over 150 funders from around the world, the Indiegogo crowdfunding campaign to fund this project was a huge success. Early momentum had nearly half the goal met within forty-eight hours of launch, and overall contributions ranged from $1 to $3,500. I am extremely grateful to those individuals who helped this project become a reality.

Aside from the funding, the project became a success in another important way. The additional benefit was the enormous wave of positive feedback that was generated by the campaign.

PR-wise, Aish.com and the Canadian Jewish News were both enthusiastic about publishing campaign-related articles. Aish.com's piece, which was written by my mother about her perspective on having a child who stutters, quickly received more than 5,500 page viewings and sparked a flurry of positive comments. And the CJN's op-ed, which was featured as a full-page article in the printed version, went viral on the internet. Not only did more than 800 readers "share" the article into their social media feed, but it was also (somehow) picked up by The National Stuttering Foundation, who posted it on their Facebook page — a post which quickly scored more than 500 "Likes" and many positive comments.

It was also great to hear from Slava Rubin, CEO at Indiegogo (the platform I used for the crowdfunding campaign), about how much he appreciated my campaign — not just because it was successful in hitting its goal, but because it was also helping a meaningful cause.

In addition, I began to receive e-mails from people all around the world. People who stuttered reached out for my advice, while many other people commended me for sharing my story. And inasmuch as I made myself publicly vulnerable through my struggle with adversity, I found that many others responded in kind, with people sharing with me different challenges that they have faced.

I started working on this project around three years ago. The overwhelmingly enthusiastic response when I launched the campaign reinforced the need for my book and validated spending the necessary additional time it would take to get it into bookstores worldwide. I was reminded that everyone is faced with challenges. Be it a stutter or otherwise, adversity can make it difficult to achieve true happiness and can seriously call into question one's relationship with G-d.

Therefore, as I concluded my campaign and started working with my publisher to complete the manuscript, I began to feel a deep sense of humility and satisfaction knowing that my story has the potential to help many other people in their quest to find meaning, purpose, and true happiness amidst their challenges — whatever they may be.

The following people (among others who prefer to remain anonymous) generously made this book possible. May they be blessed in all areas of their lives, and particularly with the privilege of continuing to perpetuate goodness in the world.

Dedicated by

the Volfson family

in loving memory

of

Robbie's father,

Mordechai ben Chaim Leib

Dedicated

by

Barry & Aleta Shiff & family

In honor

of

Moe & Melanie Mernick & family

Mazel tov on the realization and dream of completing your book.

Your journey and story will touch and inspire many.

We are very proud of you.

Love,

Bubie Millie and Saba Howard

*I am thrilled to see this book published
and humbled to support its emergence.
In the American spirit of freedom
of speech...
In the Jewish value of freedom
to be who you are,
fulfilling your life's purpose
with your unique skill set
and personal circumstances...
And in friendship and admiration
of Moe Mernick and his family.*

**Dena and Uri
and the Schneider family**

Dear Moshe,

It took great courage to write this book. You have SO much to be proud of, and you accomplished more in your twenty-something years than most people achieve in a lifetime. You are a role model to all who know you, young and old. We look forward to following your success in the future, and may you realize all your dreams and endeavors. Continue to reach high, because you are surely gifted in every way. Good luck. You are truly VERY special.

Fran & Stan Ages

Dear Moshe,

I treasure every moment I spend with you and every conversation we have together. You are a true example of a talmid chacham and a wonderful friend.
Mazel tov on this wonderful achievement, the first book of many, I have no doubt.

By telling your story, you have committed to writing your life's message. That Hashem runs the show and that the challenges we face in life are not random, but unique gifts sent to each of us so that we may overcome them and ultimately grow stronger.
May this book inspire all its readers in a way that you inspire all those who have the pleasure of knowing you.

In memory of my dear father-in-law whom I had the privilege of knowing for a short time before his untimely death. A true talmid chacham, the words of Torah were forever on his lips. A man who always saw the good in life and made the world a better place for all those who knew him.
We miss him very much.

E. A. Cohen

Dear Moshe,

We are humbled and awed by your strength and determination, from a delicious little boy to an accomplished young man...and this is only the beginning.

We look forward to continuing to shep nachas as we observe you on your much applauded journey forward.

With tremendous pride,

Yossi and Chaya Salamon

Yashar Koach, Moshe, on this wonderful accomplishment

You are an inspiration — not only to all those who deal with the challenge of stuttering, but to anyone who deals with any physical or mental challenge.

Your ability, even at a young age, to appreciate that you were given this test, not just for you to pass, but for a greater purpose, is incredible. It gave you the ability to not only embrace this challenge yourself, but to turn the experience and the knowledge into an opportunity to help others embrace their challenges.

Your courage, determination, commitment, independence, and perseverance are remarkable.

Keep inspiring us and all of the people that are blessed to know you.

Mitch, Paula, Joshua, and Brandon Silverstein
Aryeh, Tziviah, and Sari Mernick

"Make a teacher for yourself and acquire a friend." A dictum from our Sages that is often difficult to fulfill. Fortunate is the one who finds both a teacher and true friend in the same person. Thank you for always guiding, teaching, and leading by example throughout our friendship.

Benyamin Moss

Dedicated to our children and grandchildren and future generations — may we be blessed with the merit to live a life of *simchah* and *shalom* in Eretz Yisrael with all the Jewish People united in Hashem's glory.

Dedicated by the very proud in-laws,

Aryeh & Miriam Deverett

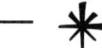

Moshe,

Words cannot adequately express how fortunate I feel to have you as a brother. You have always been a source of unwavering support, a pillar of strength, and a close friend. I am delighted to know that those who have not had the privilege of having you in their lives will now get the opportunity to be inspired by you as well.

With love and admiration,

Yoni

I dedicate this page in honor of the author's incredible dearth of simple vocabulary words found in the English language. For example: He never said "I can't," "impossible," and "why me?" even from the young age that I had the great fortune of having him as a friend, then as an inspiration, and finally as a hero in my life. I know you will remember us "little people" as you grow from success to success!

With deep admiration,

Ari & Naomi Bensoussan

To live your life with passion is commendable, to show others how to do the same is exceptional.

Stay inspired and keep inspiring.

Daniel

Rabbi Mernick,

May everyone that you meet and influence recognize, as we do, you strength of character, kindness, and sincere love for humankind.
It is a privilege to be able to call you our friend, and it is with honesty that we consider you a role model. With the warmest and most heartfelt of *berachos* for unmitigated success in every imaginable way,

Elchanan & Sara Shoff

I'd like to thank the author and my colleague,
Moe Mernick.

Moe, you are a truly positive, interesting, and admirable person, and many of my days have been uplifted by your optimism since we met.

Your energy is contagious and I hope you continue to infect people at work and beyond.

With appreciation,

Yudi Levi

To my good friend, *chavruta*, and mentor, Moshe Mernick, with gratitude for all of the Torah and inspiration you share with me. I wish you much *hatzlachah* in all your endeavors and look forward with excitement to reading your book and continuing to learn from you.

The Mitchells

In honor of all those with speech impediments, as well as the speech therapists without whom our difficulties would be so much greater.

Anonymous

Dedicated in memory of our beloved father
R' Yisroel Chaim ben R' Dovid
Mr. Irwin Peyser

Renee and Eli Singer

In loving memory of Howard R. Woolf (Haskal ben Shmuel), *a"h*, who overcame similar challenges in his life. He devoted his life to selfless caring and giving to others less fortunate. We can all learn from his example. May his soul be elevated in the merit of this book and dedication.

Heidi & Baruch Bergenfeld

This revolutionary firsthand account is a tremendous leap forward in educating others about the struggles of stuttering. Through this inspirational story, we can better relate and relay this knowledge to help others in our community. This story also shows individuals with struggles that they, too, can persevere, be proactive, and inspire others.

This dedication is in memory of Eva Ochs, who exemplified a true and devoted educator for all kinds of learners.

**Elana and David Ochs,
owners of Kol Chaverim Preschool**

Dedicated to Leah Chaya Ruzanova (*ob"m*), a devoted mother and grandmother.

With love,

Mascha, Avraham Yitzchak, Hillel Aharon, Nachum Benyamin, and Sarah Shuva Radbil

To my precious wife, Beth:

You continue to take such good care of our family while growing steadily greater.

May we continue to be a helpful team to Hashem until age 120.

Love,

Moshe Firestone

In loving memory of our dear grandparents:

Francine Elkins

Rabbi Irving and Amy Frankel

Emil and Eva Katz

David and Rica Rubinstein

Aaron & Molly Katz

AND THANKS TO...

Aaron Ishida	Benjamin Gliklich	Elana & Eitan Borvick
Adam Aranov	Caryl Rothberg	Eli & Natalie Menaged
Adi Karmon Scope	Cédric & Naomi Bollag	Eli & Shani Neumann
Alex, Rachel & Ariel Zveiris	Chavi Gestetner	Family Sajatz
Amy & David Weinberg	Cynthia Bernstein	Fihrer family
Amy & Shalom Schwartz and family	Daniel & Esther Yormark	Gareth & Esther Jankelow
Ari & Rochel Waldman	Danny & Sandi Brager	Hanan Hurwitz
Arthur Rabinovitch	David & Eve Kerzner	Harris family
Aryeh & Tziviah Mernick	David Garcia	Ian Zeifman
Auntie Laurie	Devorah Deverett	Jamie Azoulay
AY & Sarah Mernick	Doreen (Dori) Lenz Holte	Jay Deverett
Barry Greengart	Dorit & Shai Sfadyah	Jeremy Hurewitz
Bean family	Dovid & Shana Aaronson	Josh Manger
Ben & Ellie Menora	Dovid Rose	Judy Levine
Ben Flom	Dvorah Prince, M.S., CCC-SLP	Kasriel Stewart

Kenny & Sherri Wise	Rabbi Ari & Shayna Enkin	Shira & Mordechai Yormark
Larry & Natalie Froom	Rabbi Rafi & Shira Lipner	Shira & Scott Sheps
Lynnie & David Mirvis	Rabbi Samuel Ross	Shmuel & Shana Herman
Mark Feld	Rabbi Yisrael & Hindy Motzen and family	Simon Benninga
Meir Mittel	Rabinowitz family	Simon Italiaander
Menzelefsky family	Rachelle Shapiro	Tak
Michal & Baruch Moskoff	Rafi & Malkie Allman	Talia Krause
Michal & Yonatan Frankel	Reuven & Chave Jacobsohn	Tamar Warburg Gross
Miriam & Moti Balla	Ronald & Marcie Sheps	The Neumann family
Moshe & Anna Grunfeld	Roy Mendel Shelef	Toby Rosner
Moshe Nadoff	Rubin family	Victor and Sara Hyman
Naftoli & Leora Klein	Sammy Polster	Yaakov & Esther Friedman
Nancy Prussky	Shalva & Sruli Weinreb	Yechiel Weisz
Nathan Light	Shev & Haysha Shatzman	Yoav Shans
Noam Ben-Ari, M.S CCC-SLP	Shimon & Shoshana Newman and family	Zalmi, Leah & Estie Finn
Rabbi & Mrs. Doniel Ginsberg	Shimon Yaakov	Zuckerman family

ABOUT THE AUTHOR

Combining both of his passions, Jewish education and entrepreneurship, Moe Mernick runs International Marketing for an early-stage start-up, mentors budding entrepreneurs at a Jerusalem-based technology accelerator and has held numerous Jewish communal positions, including Regional Director for The Ronald S. Lauder Foundation (Hamburg, Germany), Senior Advisor at Counterpoint (Sydney, Australia) and City Director for NCSY (Vancouver, Canada). Moe holds an International MBA and Rabbinical Ordination, and lives in Israel with his wife and children.

Moe would be happy to hear from readers. You may personally reach out to him with any questions or comments by writing to moemernick@gmail.com.

ABOUT MOSAICA PRESS

Mosaica Press is an independent publisher of Jewish books. Our authors include some of the most profound, interesting, and entertaining thinkers and writers in the Jewish community today. There is a great demand for high-quality Jewish works dealing with issues of the day — and Mosaica Press is helping fill that need. Our books are available around the world. Please visit us at www.mosaicapress.com or contact us at info@mosaicapress.com. We will be glad to hear from you.

MOSAICA PRESS